The Power of Peace Within Me

Mindful Yoga for Healing

Lynn Williams, PhD

Table of Contents

Foreword 1

Following Your True Life Path 3

CHAPTER 1
Real Power Is Within You 5
- Skill Sheet: Who Do You Think You Are? Core Beliefs 6
- My Goals 7
- Mountain Pose 8
- Conscious Breathing 9
  - Restorative Practice: Breath Awareness 9

CHAPTER 2
Choosing Happiness 11
- Skill Sheet: Your Life Diamond: Core Values 12
- Things in Your Control 13
- Warrior 1 Pose 14
- Daily Meditation Practice 15
  - Restorative Practice: Hand Over the Heart 15

CHAPTER 3
Go with the Flow of Life 17
- Skill Sheet: Mindfulness Skills 18
- Reflect on What You Have Control Over 19
- Lying Down Pose 20
- Yogic Breathing 21
  - Restorative Practice: Open Palms 21

CHAPTER 4
Being in the Present Moment 23
- Skill Sheet: Self-Check of Stress 24
- Flexibility 25
- Cat-Cow Pose 26
- Restorative Practice: Full Body Relaxation 27

CHAPTER 5
Letting Go of Negativity 33
Skill Sheet: Distract and Self-Soothe 35
- Skill Sheet: Self-Soothe with the 5 Senses 36
- Self-Forgiveness 37
- Downward Triangle Pose 38
- Expanding Awareness of the Breath 39
  - Restorative Practice: 4-7-8 Breath 39

CHAPTER 6
Cultivating Patience 41
Skill Sheet: ACT, Don't React: Skills for Tough Times 42
Break Free of Negative Patterns 43
Standing Forward Fold Pose 44
Deep Relaxation Breathing 45
Restorative Practice: Palming the Eyes 45

CHAPTER 7
The True Purpose of Your Life 47
Skill Sheet: Reviewing Your Day 48
Your Reason for Being 49
Child's Pose 50
Breathing to Relieve Stress 51
Restorative Practice: Bumblebee Breath 51

CHAPTER 8
Love Is the Answer 53
Skill Sheet: Activities You Enjoy 54
Your Gratitude List 55
Bridge Pose 56
Alternate Nostril Breathing 57
Restorative Practice: Legs up the Wall 57
Sound Meditation Technique 58

CHAPTER 9
We Need Each Other 61
Skill Sheet: MINDFUL Skill 62
Skill Sheet: Create MEANING Skill 63
Centering Practice 64
Plank Pose 65
Meditation Stopping the War Within 66
Restorative Practice: Healing Light Meditation 67
Youth Testimonials 68

CHAPTER 10
Yoga off the Mat 71
Your Life Destination 72
Body Twist Pose 73
Walking Meditation 74
Breath of Joy 74
Finding Peace: Dealing with Grief and Loss 75
Restorative Practice: Calming Touch 75

Reviewing Our Life Values 76
Talk the Talk, Walk the Walk 77
Further Reading 79
Yoga F.L.A.M.E. 80
Top Ten Benefits of Yoga 82
Acknowledgements 83
Practice with Us! Yoga Companion DVD 84

Foreword

I am so pleased that Dr. Lynn Williams has created this beautiful companion guide to my book **Yoga: A Path for Healing and Recovery.** She has done a masterful job of relating the true intention of yoga, all of its aspects, and how it can be applied to the challenges in everyday lives with ***The Power of Peace Within Me.*** I look at yoga as an age-old personal development practice that if taken to heart has the potential to change your life. Anybody who has embraced a yoga practice and stuck with it can speak to the support it has given them in dealing with personal difficulties. One of the participants in my program at San Quentin Prison put it this way:

> "My yoga practice has helped me with impulse control, obsessive and compulsive thinking patterns, and given me the ability to find calm in stressful situations. I have learned what it means to be at peace with myself and live everyday mindful of who I really am."

There is no greater gift that you can give to yourself than peace of mind. Money cannot buy it. It's something that you have to nurture for yourself through willpower and effort. And like anything that is worthwhile in life, it requires practice. Now you have the perfect guide for practicing with ***The Power of Peace Within Me.*** It offers practical tools and simple exercises to support the power within you, relieve the stress of everyday life, and improve your physical and emotional health. I hope you use it as the gift Dr. Williams intends it to be for inner peace and your overall well-being.

Namaste,

James Fox
Founding Director

Following Your True Life Path

Hello and welcome! We start our yoga classes saying "Namaste," which means "The light in me honors the light within you." In yoga, even though we have our differences, we honor the same light that is within all of us. We are so happy you picked up this guide and hope the teachings help you connect with your highest Self and live a more joyful, peaceful life.

Yoga means "union," and practicing yoga brings together body, mind, and spirit in holistic unity and alignment. Beginning with a theme and a statement of affirmation, each chapter includes skill sheets, reflection/journaling exercises, a yoga word of the week, restorative exercises to help rebalance and reset the mind-body system, and a suggested activity to contribute to the well-being of another. Stressors in life can deplete our energy resources, leaving us like a cell phone battery that needs to be recharged.

The restorative exercises are designed to do just that: help you recharge, reset, and restore your mind-body system for a happier, healthier you. Through the suggested activities, we learn the practice of "Karma Yoga". These exercises of selflessness involve doing positive things for others without any thought of recognition, reward, or repayment for ourselves.

While you are practicing the poses, please pay attention to your body, and stop if you feel any pain. Please check with your doctor if you are pregnant, have high blood pressure, or have a heart condition before starting your yoga practice.

I have personally witnessed yoga and meditation help so many young people open to their true potential at the juvenile prisons and detention centers where I have worked. For this book, I picked exercises and activities that these students told me were helpful to them. I have been so grateful for the opportunities to share, heal and grow together with them through this practice of yoga.

I hope you have fun with this guide. May your yoga practice be an exploration into who you truly are. May this practice serve to light the lamp within you and help you share that beautiful light with others. Humanitarian and Gandhi-King Award for Non-Violence winner Amma (Mata Amritanandamayi) shares this wish for our lives:

"May the tree of our life be firmly rooted in the soil of love.
May good deeds be the leaves on that tree.
May words of kindness form its flowers,
and may peace be its fruit."

May the love and peace created within our hearts extend to everyone around the world. Together, may we come one step closer to greater peace and harmony within our ourselves and in our world. May our thoughts, words, and actions have one goal: that all beings be peaceful, happy, and truly free.

Dr. Lynn Williams
Prison Yoga Project,
Northern Ohio Juvenile Program

The Prison Yoga Project, founded in 2002 by James Fox, is an amazing program that helps thousands of prisoners learn yoga in order to better deal with difficulties in their lives and manage their emotions while incarcerated. His book, Yoga: A Path for Healing and Recovery, gives a comprehensive outline of all the important concepts of yoga that help people connect with who they truly are and, from that place, make changes in their lives.

This guide ends with a "Further Reading" page (p.79) that pairs each chapter with various exercises from his book to deepen your practice. The goal is for you to take your yoga "off the mat" and apply the teachings in your daily life. You will build skills to make better choices, improve the way you manage your emotions and relationships, help your community, and benefit our world.

If you are incarcerated, you can request a copy of his book free of charge from the address on page 83.

CHAPTER 1

Real Power Is Within You

"I am powerful beyond measure.
I am awesome."

What does it look like to be powerful?

If we look at television or the internet, we might that think having lots of money, cars, and fancy things makes us powerful. However, these external things and temporary pleasures do not give us real power or lasting happiness. I am sure we can all think of celebrities who have a lot of money but suffer from depression, or alcohol/drug addictions and may even have tried to commit—or committed—suicide. Clearly, although they might have been perceived as powerful by society's standards, they were not at peace within themselves. True power is not from external things but from what is inside ourselves. Yoga is a path to help us go deeper inward and to explore the true treasures we already possess within, for it is this which leads to true and lasting happiness.

By developing our "inner guide" or "true self" we can break free from negative behaviors that might make us feel good temporarily but actually take away our real power. Being in prison may magnify our feelings of powerlessness. This may cause a tendency to engage in negative behaviors that seem to increase our sense of power, but actually accomplish the opposite while creating more stress and negativity.

What negative behaviors have you used to deal with stress that actually caused you more stress and problems in the end?

____

____

____

What goals do you have for yourself as you start this yoga practice?

____

____

____

____

Who Do You Think You Are?

Core Beliefs

Let's look more closely at our beliefs about ourselves.

Check the negative beliefs we may have about ourselves.

Core Negative Beliefs About Ourselves:

"Lies I Tell Myself"

- ❒ I am not good enough.
- ❒ I can't do it.
- ❒ I am unsuccessful.
- ❒ I am worthless.
- ❒ I am unlovable.
- ❒ I am unacceptable.
- ❒ I am not special.
- ❒ I am no good.
- ❒ I don't belong.
- ❒ I am unwanted.
- ❒ I am uninteresting.
- ❒ I am unattractive.
- ❒ I am stupid.
- ❒ I don't deserve anything.
- ❒ Something is wrong with me.

Now check the positive beliefs we may have about ourselves.

Core Positive Beliefs About Ourselves:

"The Truth of Who I Am"

- ❒ I am likeable.
- ❒ I am lovable.
- ❒ I am smart.
- ❒ I am special.
- ❒ I am attractive.
- ❒ I am proud of who I am.
- ❒ I am just as worthy as others.
- ❒ I am awesome.
- ❒ I am successful.
- ❒ I deserve love.
- ❒ I have courage to face difficulties.
- ❒ I am in control.
- ❒ I deserve to be happy.
- ❒ I can succeed.
- ❒ I am strong.

YOU'RE A SUPER STAR

Change It Up: More Positivity, Please!

Now, rewrite the negative beliefs you struggle with the most into positive beliefs that are just for you. For example, if you checked "I am unsuccessful," you might write, "I can do anything I put my mind to, and I will succeed."

Say these positive affirmations throughout the day as often as you can.

____

____

____

____

Return to Center—Time to Reflect

Michael Jordan said, "I've missed more than 9000 shots in my career. I've lost almost 300 games. Twenty-six times, I've been trusted to take the game-winning shot and missed. I've failed over and over and over again in my life. And that is why I succeed." He never gave up because he knew his goals and believed in himself. Sometimes, we make negative choices because, deep down, we hold negative beliefs about ourselves. He had a positive belief about himself and knew that he could do it if he kept trying. This is called a core positive belief. If he had not believed in himself, he would have thought, "I tried, but I can't do it. I give up." Positive beliefs help us keep trying even though we might feel like we failed and just want to give up.

Write YOUR goals on the lines below.

My Goals:

Short-Term Goals (you can accomplish daily or weekly)

____

____

____

____

Long-Term Goals (you can accomplish monthly or yearly)

____

____

____

____

Make sure your short-term goals are specific steps that are working toward your long-term goals. By starting this yoga practice now, you will harness the skills—your REAL POWER! —needed for your body and mind to break free from negative patterns, allowing you to reach your goals.

Return to Center—Back to Our Bodies

"I stand in my center. I am focused, calm, and grounded."

Centering & Opening

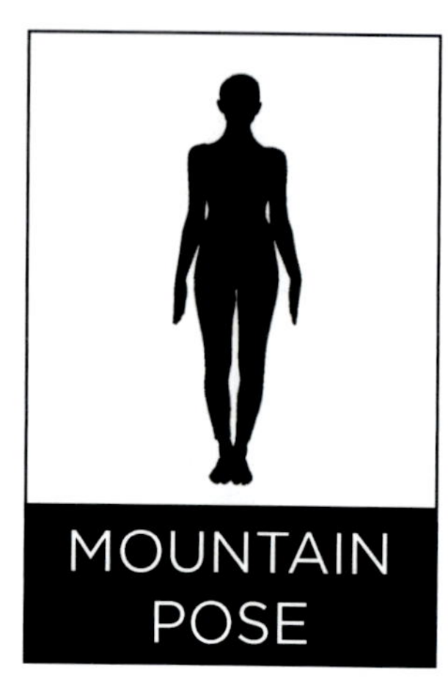
MOUNTAIN POSE

One of the first poses we learn in yoga is Mountain Pose. When you are in your center, you are grounded and strong, immovable. Yoga is about bringing together your entire mind, body, and spirit. Stand in Mountain Pose and really focus on your core positive beliefs. Say them to yourself. Notice what it feels like in your body to stand in who you truly are. Notice the bottoms of your feet making contact with the ground. Take a nice deep breath and on the exhalation say to yourself, **"I stand in my center. I am focused, calm, and grounded."** Let your weight be balanced and even. Lift up through your head. Lengthen your spine and open your shoulders. Relax your shoulders, soften your jaw, and let your tongue rest at the bottom of your mouth. Soften your eyes.

Say to yourself,
"I stand in my center.
I am focused, calm, and grounded."

Think about the differences between a sailboat and a motorboat. If you are a sailboat, you go whichever way the wind is blowing.

In our lives, if we are not in our center, we may shift with whatever is happening and whoever is around us. We might feel restless or out of control and become easily influenced—a victim of circumstances. If we stay in our center, like a motorboat, we can not be so influenced by external things. We decide which direction we want to go to achieve our goals. Stand proudly in your Mountain, in who you really are, and in your True Power!

Return to Center—Back to Our Breath

Conscious Breathing

Our breath is our life force, and simply being aware of our breath can be a tool to help us stand in our center when things are difficult.

Place your hands on your belly and take a deep breath inhaling fully. Feel your belly and lungs expand like a balloon filling up. Now exhale fully letting all the air out like a ballon deflating. Feel your stomach pull in towards your back as you breathe out. Try this a few more times.

Restorative Practice
Breath Awareness

Sit or lie down comfortably.

Place a palm on your stomach and breathe comfortably for a few moments, noticing the quality of your breath. How does your breath feel? Does the breath feel warm? Cool? Tense? Strained? Uneven? Deep? Shallow? Short? Long? Simply observe the breath without any judgment.

Gradually begin to make your breathing as relaxed and smooth as possible. As you inhale, let your stomach naturally expand like a balloon; as you exhale, feel your stomach contract like a balloon deflating. Release your hand from your stomach and simply notice your breath. Allow any thoughts or emotions to just pass by like clouds in the sky. Whenever you notice your mind wandering come back to your breath.

Continue the practice for 6 to 12 breaths.

take a deep breath

Breathe

You're Awesome (or Namaste)

In yoga, we greet each other with honoring the pure light within us that is also the same light within all beings. Simply, the meaning can be described as, "I'm awesome; you're awesome." It is a gesture of gratitude and a reminder of our oneness with each other.

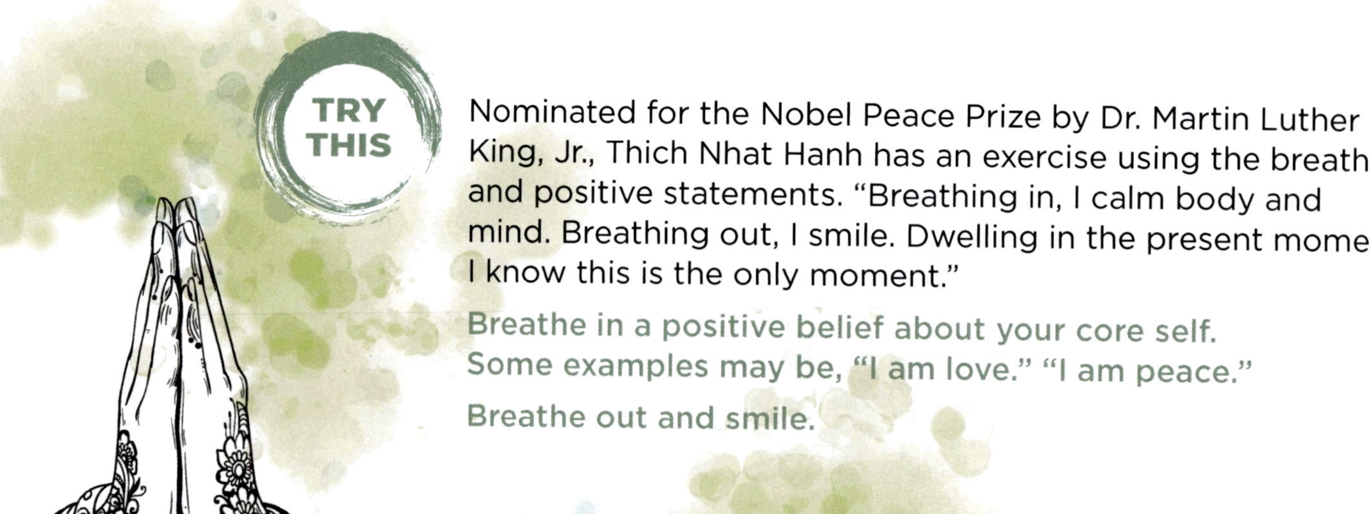

TRY THIS

Nominated for the Nobel Peace Prize by Dr. Martin Luther King, Jr., Thich Nhat Hanh has an exercise using the breath and positive statements. "Breathing in, I calm body and mind. Breathing out, I smile. Dwelling in the present moment I know this is the only moment."

Breathe in a positive belief about your core self. Some examples may be, "I am love." "I am peace."

Breathe out and smile.

CHAPTER 2

Choosing Happiness

"No matter what is happening in my life, I will stay strong and choose happiness."

Now that we know where our true power lies, we can become more grounded in the true self when we look at our core values. Yoga is about living our lives in line with our core values and making each thought, word, and action an expression of who we really are.

Complete the exercise titled "Your Life Diamond" on the next page so you can look at the positive things about YOU! These strengths are unique to you, as there is only one YOU in this world, and now is your time to shine like a diamond! When you look at your values try to focus on who you are and what you have rather than what you do not have. Take a minute to be grateful for the things you already have that support you and give you the encouragement and strength to make positive choices when times are difficult. When we become overstressed or make poor choices, we might choose negative behaviors that cause us more stress and problems. These are times when we have forgotten who we are and what our core life values are.

Remembering our core values, we can stay firm in our center—our Truth, our true power—no matter what opposing forces or challenging life circumstances we may encounter. Our core values are our inner compass, our inner guide, the teacher within.

Mindfulness helps us stay aware so we can maintain our true life direction and communication with our inner guide. Mindfulness is key in both our yoga practice and in our everyday lives. Throughout the day, we may encounter many ups and downs, many happy times and sad times. The problem is that we can get caught up in the swirl of thoughts and emotions in our minds. Just like the movement of the ocean, they can be crashing waves or low, gentle ripples, but our restless minds are always moving. Underneath the waves lies a stillness found only at the bottom of the ocean.

Yoga with mindful awareness trains your mind to stay centered, calm, and still by helping you take a step back from your thoughts and emotions. By putting your focus back on your body and breath, you can stay peaceful and balanced no matter what is going on in your life.

SKILL SHEET

Your Life Diamond

Circle the things that represent you, or write in your own:

Your Core Values, (Your Priorities):

- Family
- Friends
- Health
- Education
- Career
- Spirituality
- Relationships
- Fun
- Laughter
- Recreation

What prevents you from shining?

- Using drugs
- Poor anger management
- Drinking
- Isolating
- Risk-taking behaviors
- Getting into fights
- Negative relationships
- Ignoring problems
- Self-injurious behaviors
- Making poor choices

Return to Center—Time to Reflect

Make a list of things in your life that are NOT in your control.

____

____

____

Now make a list of things that ARE in your control.

____

____

____

How can you spend more time and energy on things that are in your control?

____

____

____

What feelings arise when you feel like things are not in your control?

____

____

____

How can you let the feelings be there without pushing them away?

____

____

____

Return to Center—Back to Our Bodies

"I know who I am, and I stay calm and focused in all that I do."

Resiliency

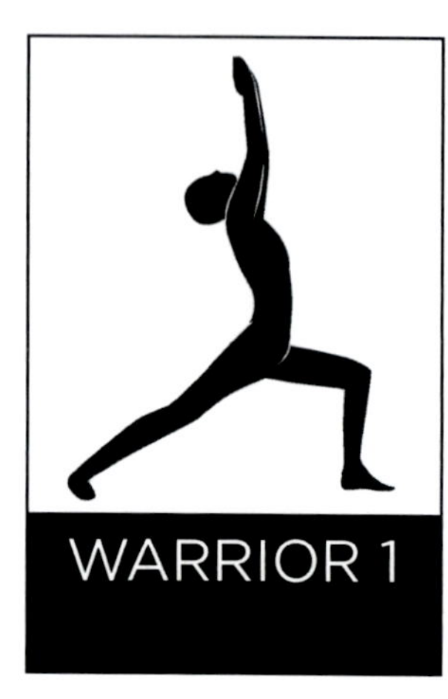

Stand in Warrior I position and breathe in a positive affirmation about yourself. For example, "I am strong." Breathe into your Warrior. Feel your balance, strength, and center. Notice what you stand for in life. Stand firm, not letting what happens in your life control how you think and feel. Take a nice deep breath, and, on the exhalation, say to yourself, **"I know who I am, and I stay calm and focused in all that I do."** Allow your mind to stay in mindful awareness. Breathe into your center, stay grounded, and don't let yourself get distracted. Now try the other side and say to yourself **"I know who I am, and I stay calm and focused in all that I do."**

Say to yourself,
"I know who I am, and I stay calm and focused in all that I do."

When we react to what is happening around us—life circumstances or people—we can give away our power and also our happiness. For example, maybe we lost someone we care about. Mindful awareness helps us not stay apart from feelings of anger or sadness but to breathe into and really feel those feelings—not becoming overwhelmed by them but instead simply letting them rise and fall. Breathe into your strong Warrior stance. From this place of peace we can begin to heal from the pain and continue to move forward in our life in a positive direction.

Return to Center—Back to Our Breath

Daily Meditation Practice

Research has shown that it takes 21 days to make something a habit. Challenge yourself, and see if you can make meditation a daily practice for 21 days! Notice your breath effortlessly flowing in and out. Try to let go of your thoughts. You might imagine your thoughts as clouds floating in the sky. Come back to your gentle breath and let your body be relaxed.

Restorative Practice

Hand Over the Heart

Sit or lie down comfortably. Put your left hand on the center of your chest (often called the "heart center") and place the thumb of your right hand in the hollow of your belly button, allowing your right palm to rest on your stomach. If you feel comfortable, close your eyes, or just keep your eyes open. Let yourself gently breathe in and out. As you notice your breath flowing in and out, feel the comfort of the warm touch of your hands. Feel the gentle pressure of your hands relax your body and calm your mind. Let this soothing touch release any tension or stress. Let yourself fully enjoy this present moment.

Yoga means "union." It is to "unite" or to make whole the mind, body, and spirit. Even more than that, yoga means to connect to our highest Self, each other, our environment, and our Truth.

Breathe in a positive core value about yourself. For example, "I am peace."

Breathe out positive thoughts to someone you care about, such as, "I wish you peace."

Breathe in another positive statement: "I am love."

Breathe out positive thoughts to someone you don't like, such as, "I wish you love." Breathe through the uncomfortable feelings and focus on who you really are.

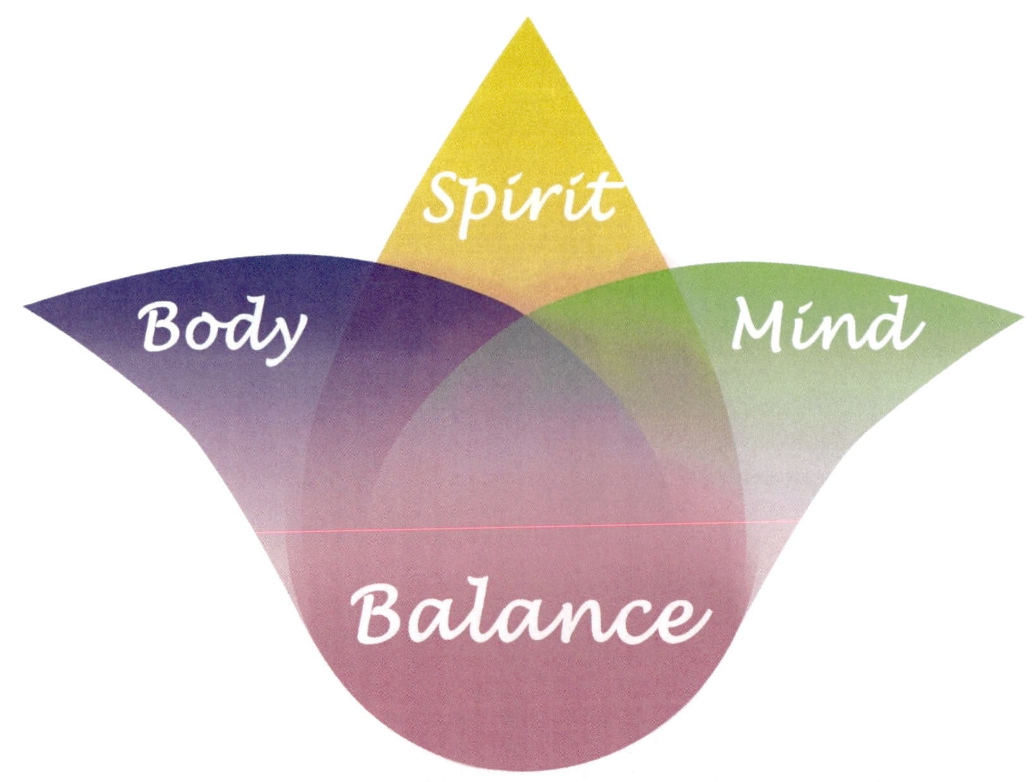

CHAPTER 3

Go with the Flow of Life

"I let go and trust the process of life; I have faith."

Even when we are centered in our core life values and positive beliefs in our true self, life may present challenges, disappointments, and heartaches that can disrupt our life flow. Remember that our breath is our life energy, our power. Conscious breathing allows us to harness our life force energy in and through the body, giving attention to and using the breath.

By coordinating the breath with yoga's physical poses, we can remove any blocks to our life force. When we can navigate challenges on the yoga mat and bring more inner balance by coordinating the breath, we are better equipped to meet life's challenges off the mat. So even if things are not going our way, the flow of our breath—our life force—is not disrupted.

By breathing fully, we distribute that powerful life force—all that wonderful oxygen—to nourish every cell, heal the body, and calm the mind. Even when things are tough, we can breathe into this state, no matter what we are faced with. We cannot control everything in our lives, but we must focus on what is in our control. We have control over ourselves and our breath.

With mindfulness, we can have greater awareness and control over our lives. Look at the "Mindfulness Skills" worksheet on the next page, and see if you can practice more self-awareness and observation rather than judging and interpreting. With this type of inner awareness, we can better go with the flow of life and have more peace and harmony within, no matter what life challenges we may face.

SKILL SHEET

Mindfulness Skills

1 Awareness

- One thing at a time
- 5 senses:

2 Be Nonjudgmental

- Don't label things as either "good" or "bad"
- Have self-compassion

3 Being in the Present Moment

- Don't think about the past or worry about the future. Be here NOW
- Actively participate in your experience, don't just "go through the motions" or "be stuck on auto-pilot"

4 Beginner's Mind

- Be open to new possibilities

Practicing Mindfulness

Mindfulness takes practice. Some people may put aside time to practice being mindful of their breath or thoughts. However, you can bring mindful awareness to any activity you do; it's particularly effective to practice with tasks you often perform without thinking, such as eating, washing dishes, cooking, taking a shower or bath, walking, driving in the car, or listening to music. In this practice the goal is not to finish the activity but to fully experience mindfulness in the moment. For example, while taking a shower you are not just wandering in your thoughts while mindlessly washing your body. You are mindfully noticing the feel of the water and warmth on your body, being grateful that you have warm water, smelling the soap, and letting go of any thoughts about the past or planning for the future. As you go about your day, try to find as many opportunities as you can to practice mindfulness while engaged in an activity.

Mindfulness is about being completely in touch with the present moment and being open to experiences as they come.

Return to Center—Time to Reflect

What are some inconvenient surprises, roadblocks, or other obstacles in your life that have come up?

____

____

____

Let go of what you do not have control over. How can you graciously flow around these challenges?

____

____

____

Focus on what you have control over.

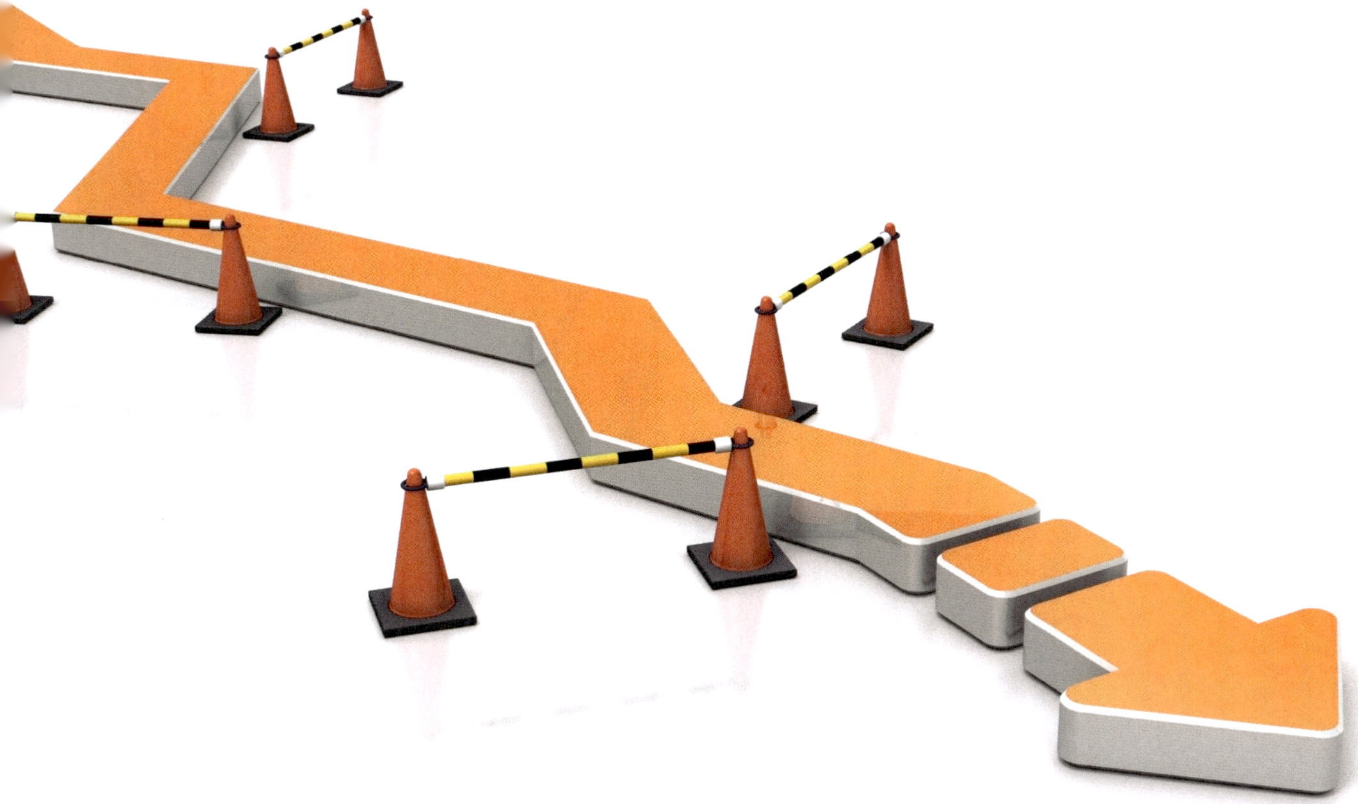

Return to Center—Back to Our Bodies

"As I relax my body and mind, I feel more peace in my heart."

Closing & Integration

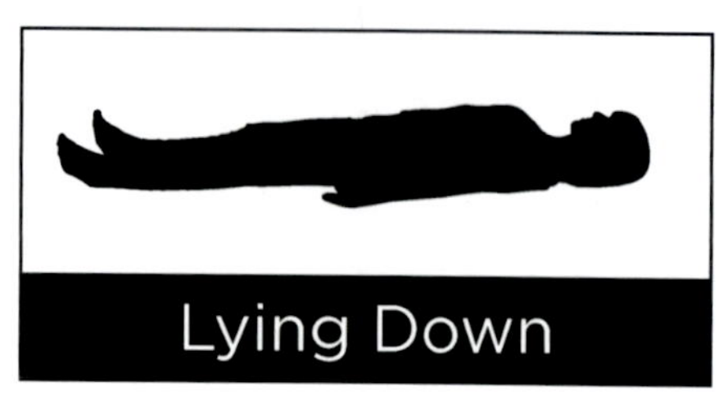

Allow yourself to fully let go of any physical tensions and mental worries in this pose. Let go of the past; you cannot change it. Let go of the future; you cannot control it. Let yourself fully be in this present moment. Inhale relaxation. Exhale stress or tension. Notice how your body feels, and say to yourself, **"As I relax my body and mind, I feel more peace in my heart."**

We need to trust the process of life and have faith that things will work out the way they are supposed to. Through yoga and breath exercises, we can be better equipped to find ways to smoothly and graciously flow around whatever difficulties arise. We can strive to accept all situations without closing our hearts or becoming afraid. We can confront the problems of life with courage and faith and let go of what no longer serves our higher purpose.

Say to yourself,

"As I relax my body and mind, I feel more peace in my heart."

Return to Center—Back to Our Breath

Yogic Breathing

Yogic breathing is also known as the "Ocean Breath." This type of breath can reduce blood pressure, calm the nervous system, and relax the mind and body. Inhale through your mouth. As you softly exhale, whisper the sound "ahhhh" through your throat area like you are fogging up a mirror. Close your mouth, but keep your lips soft. Notice the slight constriction of the throat on the inhalation and exhalation making a sound like ocean waves moving in and out.

Restorative Practice
Open Palms

Sit or lie down comfortably, allowing yourself to be aware of the breath. Experiment with closing your palms or turning them face down. What do you notice? Now turn your palms up, while keeping them open, and see what you notice. If someone is giving us a gift, we receive it with open hands. See if you can allow yourself to be open and receptive to your highest Self and the gifts in life.

Grant me the serenity to accept the things I cannot change,
the courage to change the things I can,
and the wisdom to know the difference.

Reinhold Niebuhr

Yoga emphasizes peace for your whole being—body, speech, and mind—and extends this peace to all beings in the world.

Surprise someone today.

It could be a smile, a compliment, a gift of helping or a material gift. Feel happy that you made a positive difference in someone's life.

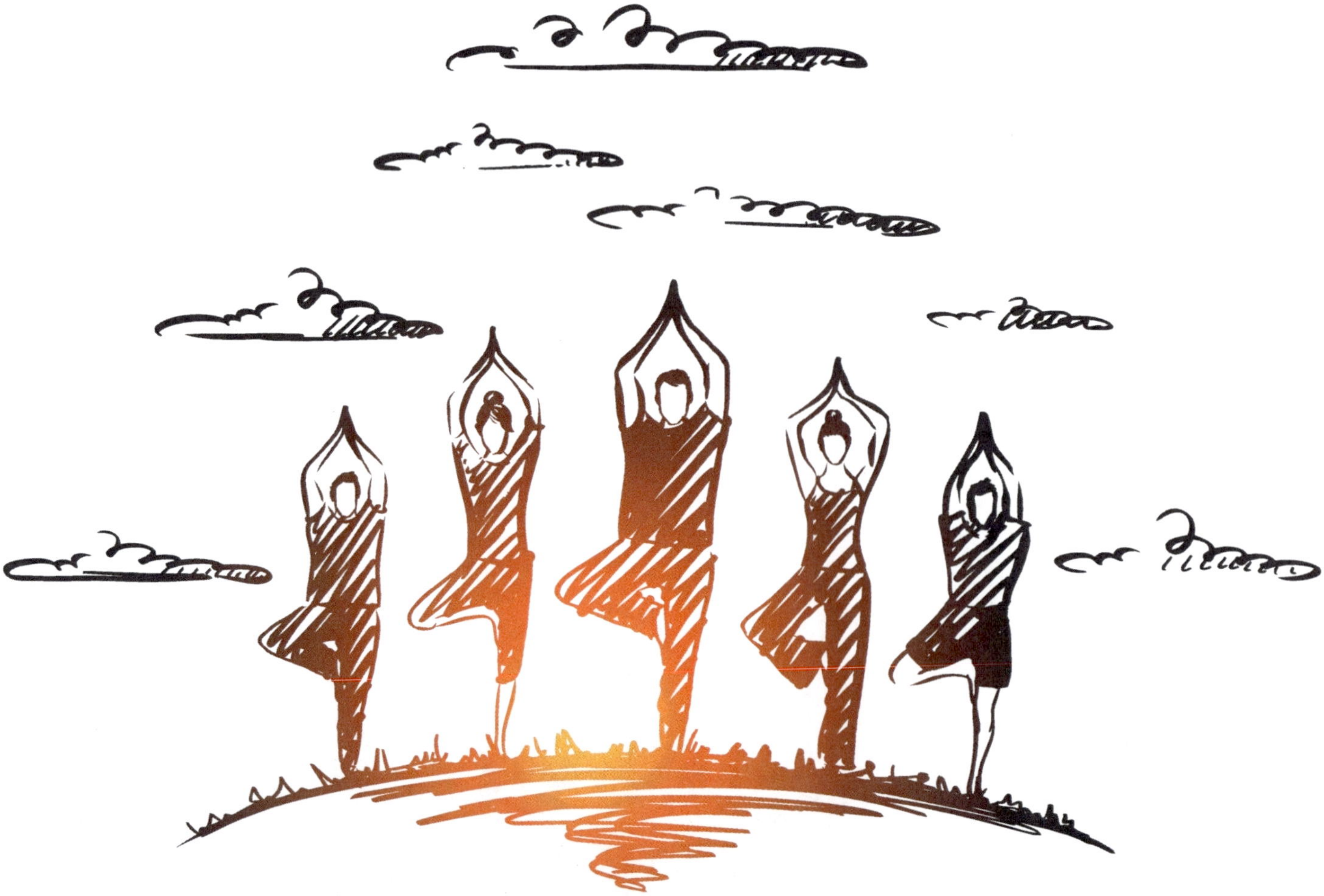

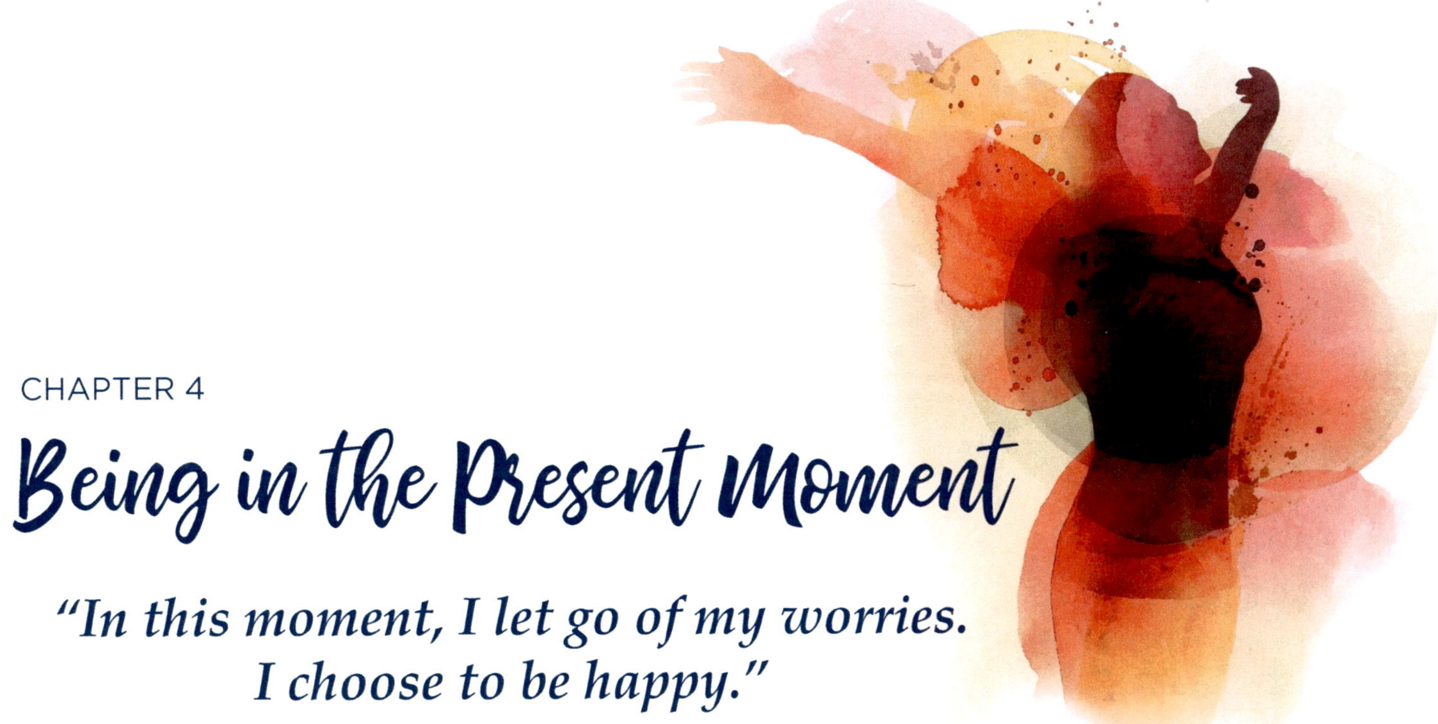

CHAPTER 4

Being in the Present Moment

"In this moment, I let go of my worries. I choose to be happy."

We may encounter many hardships in life that weigh us down and disturb our mental peace. Say we are going on a trip and have some necessary items in our backpack, such as food and water, but we also carry a few heavy rocks. Why would we continue to carry the heavy rocks on our backs if we do not need them? We would not.

The same concept applies in our lives. We need to release and fully surrender anything that weighs us down—worries, expectations, unnecessary stressors, hardships, burdens. This could include people, situations, and mistakes from our past and present life. We have to let it all go. We have to let them go.

When we let go of what we do not need, we can more fully be in the present moment. When we start our yoga practice with being in the present moment and centering, we unplug from the constant chatter of our minds, painful events from the past, and worries about the future. When we are stressed, our minds are restless and our bodies are tense. In the present moment we center and ground ourselves to the NOW through our bodies and our breath.

Look at the "Self-Check" worksheet on the next page and write down how stress feels in your body. Look at the two lines at the bottom of the worksheet together. Notice that you feel calmer when you feel more in control. The opposite is also true. The more overwhelmed you feel, the more out of control you also feel. So when you feel stressed, it's important to put your energy into things that you have control over in order to feel more at peace. For example, say we are angry at someone because they did not do something we asked them to do. We can feel angry, but we can't control other people. We can't control what they feel or what they do. We can only control ourselves. So instead of just being angry at them, we might focus on our feelings underneath the anger, such as our disappointment and hurt, and put most of our energy into ways we can manage those feelings within ourselves.

Self-Check

How does stress feel in your body?

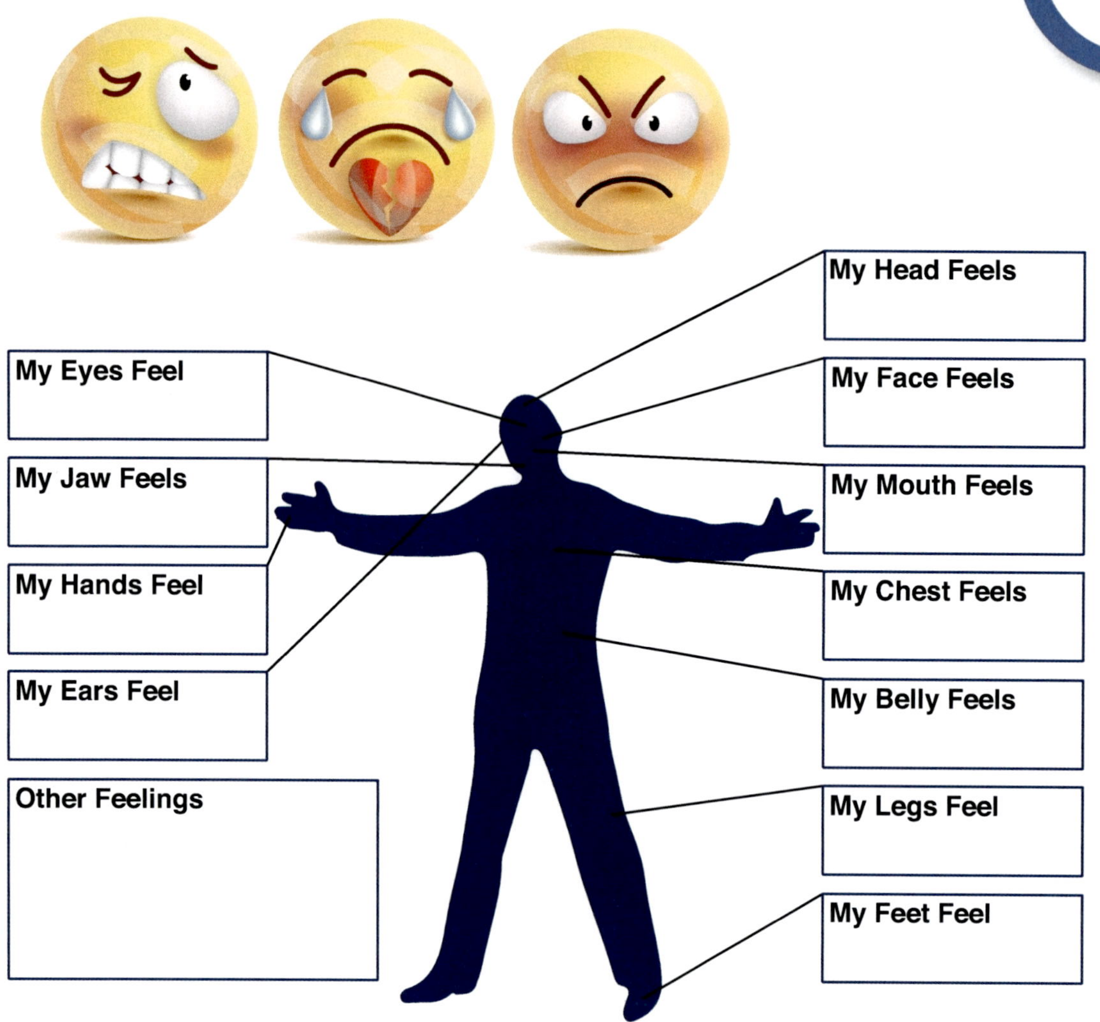

Your Body's Alarm System

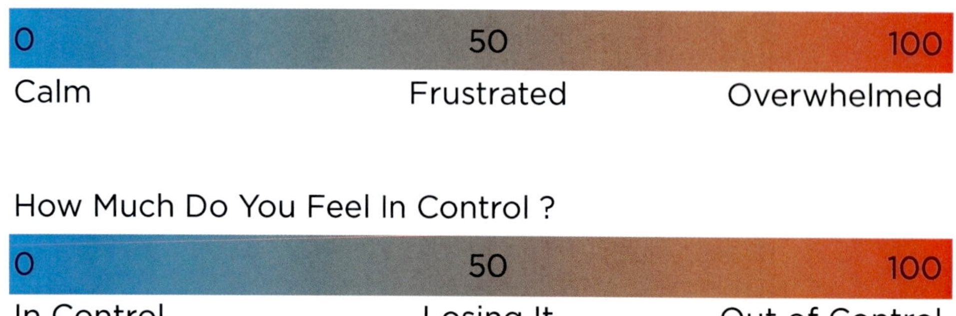

Return to Center—Time to Reflect

What are some areas in our life where we need to develop more flexibility?

____

____

____

____

By being more flexible, what positive outcomes might take place for ourselves and for others?

____

____

____

____

____

____

Return to Center, Back to Our Bodies

"I stay flexible and positive in life."

Centering & Opening

Yoga actually means to "unite" or bring together mind, body, and spirit. When you are in your center and balanced, think of being like a tree with your roots firmly in the ground. When there are storms or life challenges, the tree branches do not break, they bend. Likewise, when we face life challenges or "storms," yoga can help us more easily bend and move with life's challenges. On your hands and knees moving into Cow Pose: Inhale as you drop your belly towards the mat. Lift your chin and chest, and gaze up toward the ceiling. Broaden your shoulder blades and draw your shoulders away from your ears. Next, move into Cat Pose: As you exhale, draw your belly to your spine and round your back toward the ceiling. Flow between Cat and Cow Pose, synchronizing your inhalation and exhalation and saying to yourself, ***"I stay flexible and positive in life."***

Say to yourself,
"I stay flexible and positive in life."

Return to Center, Back to Our Breath

Restorative Practice
Full Body Relaxation

Allow yourself to let go of unnecessary stress or tension in the body and mind, making room for more peace, joy, and happiness.

Part 1:
Full Body Relaxation......Ahhhhh.....Relax

Lie down and let yourself be still. If you feel comfortable, close your eyes or, if you prefer, keep your eyes open. Allow your body to begin to relax.

Congratulate yourself for taking this time and accomplishing a step towards your goals.

Really be in this present moment.

Let go of any worries about the past. You cannot change the past.

Let go of any worries about the future. You cannot control the future. There is nothing to think about or to do; simply be in the NOW—this present moment.

Notice your breathing, watching the flow of breath come in and go out. You don't have to change the breath, just be aware of the breath flowing in.... and the breath flowing out... Scan your whole body for any tension or stress.

Inhale a deep, cleansing breath.... and exhale any tension from your body.... inhale relaxation and peace...exhale any tension and stress.

Really let it all go. Inhale relaxation and peace... exhale any tension and stress.

Now start to relax all the muscles in your body. Notice the feeling of relaxation beginning at the bottoms of your feet. It might feel like stepping into warm water, or a tingling sensation, or it might simply feel calm and loose. Allow the relaxation to spread through every toe in both of your feet and up to your ankles.

Feel the relaxation rising above your ankles, flowing up your lower legs to your knees and continuing on to your upper legs. Allow the relaxation to continue spreading throughout your body, rising now to your hips, letting your whole lower body feel relaxed. Continue to allow the relaxation to spread to your stomach and lower back to your chest and upper back. Let your upper arms relax, then your elbows, lower arms, and wrists...

Feel the relaxation spread to your hands. Relax the palms of your hands, the backs of your hands, each finger and thumb. Your hands feel warm, heavy, and relaxed.

Feel your body relaxing further as the area by your shoulders widens and relaxes. Allow your upper back to relax even further. Let your neck relax.

Feel the relaxation throughout your whole lower and upper body. Continue to spread relaxation to your chin. Relax your throat, release your jaw, relax your tongue and bring it to rest behind your bottom teeth. Let your eyes feel relaxed. Smooth out your forehead. Release any tension in the back of the neck, where the skull and neck meet. Relax your entire face. Let your entire body feel relaxed and calm.

Feel all the weight of your body settling and supported by the Earth.

Feel your body expand effortlessly into full relaxation.

Enjoy the feeling of peace within you and around you. Continue to release any other tension in the body until you feel wide open like the sky. Become thoroughly familiar with what it feels like to be open, relaxed, peaceful, and still.

Your entire body is now relaxed and calm. Feel the relaxation flowing throughout your body, from your head to your feet. Continue to relax your muscles totally, allowing the breath to flow gently out through your nose or mouth.

Allow your breath to deepen, breathing in more relaxation....and releasing any other tension in the body and mind. Now, simply relax, calmly, enjoying the feeling of peace and relaxation in the body and mind.

Part 2: Optional Extended Relaxation Visualization

Now, begin to create a picture in your mind of your safe place. Imagine a place where you feel completely comfortable and at ease.

You feel so relaxed and peaceful in this place. This might be a favorite place you have visited, or seen, or it might be completely imaginary. It's up to you. Imagine all the details this place needs in order for you to feel calm and relaxed. Start with where you are. Where is this peaceful place? You might envision somewhere outdoors or indoors. It may be a small place or a large one. Create an image of this place. It might be somewhere familiar or somewhere you have never been before. (pause)

Now, picture more details about your peaceful place. Who is in this place? Are you alone? Are there other people present? Animals? Birds? Imagine all the details of this place. (pause)

Really let yourself be in this safe place. Focus now on the relaxing sounds around you in your peaceful place. Now, imagine any tastes and smells your place has to offer. Imagine the sensations of touch, including the temperature, any breeze that may be present, and the surface you are on. Imagine the details of this calming place in your mind.

Focus now on the sights of your place—the colors, shapes, objects, plants, water—all of the beautiful things that make your place enjoyable. Really let yourself be there in this peaceful place.

What would you be doing in this calming place? Perhaps you are just sitting there, enjoying this place and relaxing. Maybe you imagine walking around a variety of activities. Picture yourself in this peaceful place. Imagine a feeling of calm, of peace. It's a place where you have no worries, cares, or concerns... a peaceful place where you can simply rejuvenate, relax, and enjoy just being. (pause)

While you are in this wonderful place, notice how you feel and how calm and happy your mind is.

Notice any affirmations that come to you as you enjoy this moment. They may be :

I am at peace with myself.

I appreciate who I am.

I value myself as a person.

I deserve to relax.

I deserve to be happy.

I release any fear, shame, or blame.

I feel relaxed and at peace in my mind, body, and soul.

I let go of any worries or burdens that I no longer need to carry.

I open my heart and surrender to the flow of life.

I embrace the present moment and will make the best of it.

I feel all my burdens being lifted.

I accept myself.

I let go of the need to control what is not in my control.

I embrace what is in my control—myself, my thoughts, my words, and my actions.

My mind is at peace and my heart is open.

By freeing myself from past mistakes, I can move on and do good things.

I forgive myself.

I imagine and believe that all of these affirmations are true for me, right now in this moment, and I enjoy the peace and relaxation I am experiencing.

I feel good about who I am today.

I can handle difficulties with grace.

I am strong.

I have faith and trust.

I can succeed.

I accept myself just the way I am.

Continue to enjoy your safe place, feeling even more confident, peaceful, and calm with the affirmations rooted deep in your heart center. Take any more time that you need to really enjoy being in this place, taking in the surroundings and how you feel.

Enjoy your peaceful place for a few moments more. Memorize the sights, sounds, and sensations around you. Know that you can return to this place in your mind's eye whenever you need a break. You can take a mental vacation to allow yourself to relax and regroup before returning to your day. In these moments of relaxation, create a picture in your mind that you will return to the next time you need a quick relaxation break. You might bring your thumb and forefinger together to bring you right back anytime you need to remember this place.

You can picture this moment you are experiencing now, anytime you need to relax.

When you are ready to return to your day, file away the place in your mind, where it will wait for you until the next time you need it.

Turn your attention back to the present, to this room, bringing with you the feelings of peace and calm. Notice your surroundings as your body and mind return to their usual level of alertness and wakefulness. You might wiggle your fingers and toes. Keep the feeling of calm from your peaceful place as you return to your everyday life. Notice how relaxed your body is. Notice the softness of your breath and the calmness of your mind. Let yourself be in this silent stillness, this perfect peace, and be grateful.

When you are ready, gently open your eyes and notice how refreshed and rejuvenated you feel, as you have brought with you peace and relaxation.

Greater Than Yourself (or Om)

In yoga we try to keep an expanded awareness that we are part of something larger than ourselves in this Universe that is always moving, always changing, and always breathing. Our breath flows in and out without our effort. The Sun rises and sets even if we do not see it. See the power of connecting with what is bigger than yourself.

TRY THIS

Smile and meet a person without judgment. Learn something new about them.

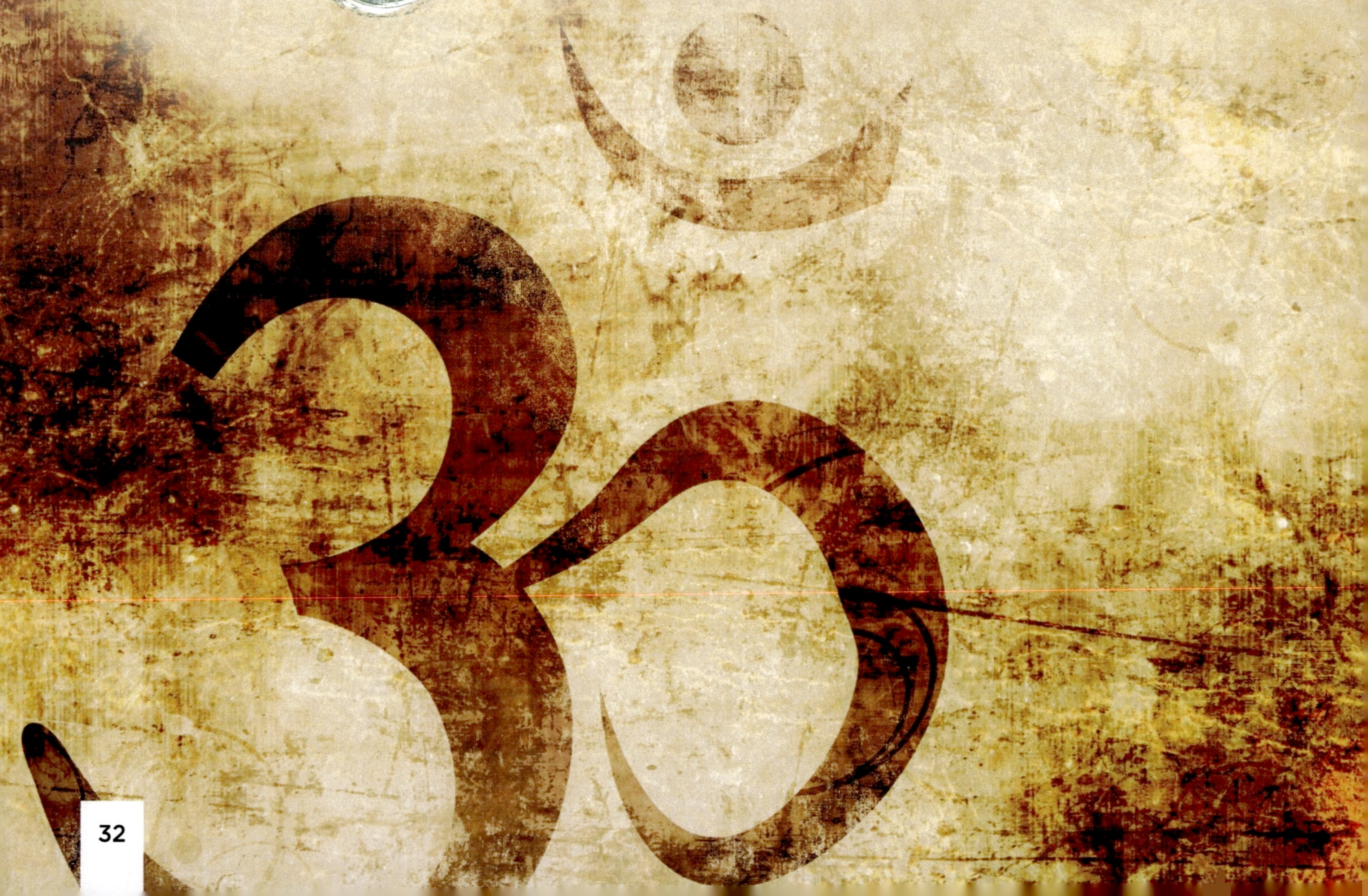

CHAPTER 5

Letting Go of Negativity

"I am strong and let go of anything that is not good for me."

When we are balanced, we are less likely to be impulsive and react to our thoughts and emotions. When we are less reactive, we have greater control over our thoughts and actions and can choose more positive ways of coping and moving closer to our life goals.

The energy centers in our bodies can be balanced or imbalanced. Negativity and negative choices can leave us in a state of imbalance. When we develop imbalances, our yoga practice uses the breath and the body to bring our energy back into a state of balance and calm. One way we might become imbalanced is by reacting in anger. Anger can be a positive or negative emotion. Let's look at fire. Fire can be used constructively (positively), by cooking food, or it can be used destructively (negatively), by burning and destroying things. Reacting in anger can leak our energy or our power, especially when we act impulsively, without thinking. Often, when we are angry, we say or do things we might regret later. If we are in balance, we can simply observe or watch our anger as it comes and goes in various situations and choose how we want to respond rather than react.

By starting to just notice our anger using our mindfulness skills, we can begin to loosen its hold on us. By sitting nonjudgmentally with our anger before reacting, we might even notice that we have painful feelings hidden underneath, such as disappointment, fear, hurt, or sadness.

By creating more space between ourselves and our emotions, we have more room to act rather than react. The distract and self-soothe skills (p. 35) allow us to

not react impulsively but, instead, take a moment to step away from our intense emotion. With this space, we can have more control over what we choose to express in our words and actions, and therefore have more control over our lives.

Go back to Chapter 2 (p. 13) in this workbook and look at the things you wrote that are and are not in your control. When things are not in our control, how do we react? Now, think of a situation that upsets you and notice what feelings you have. Give yourself some space from the emotion. Take a deep breath and just observe or "sit" with the emotion. Notice what the emotion feels like in your body. Don't try to push it away or change it, just be curious and accepting. Let the emotion be there and just label it without judgment. Notice any underlying emotions that arise as well. You might say "I accept myself feeling ________ (anger, shame, guilt, anxiety, frustration, fear, etc.)." Breathe in and out and continue to practice acceptance and self-compassion as you notice these emotions.

The next page has skills to help us let go. When we have uncomfortable emotions or challenging life situations, what are some negative behaviors we might engage in to numb and protect us from the pain?

Now take that real life situation and try not to go on "auto pilot" and react from your emotions. Try replacing a negative behavior with a "distract and self-soothe" skill and see how that works out for you. Practice makes perfect. You can do it; just breathe.

Distract and Self-Soothe

Skills to help you Let Go

You can't control all life situations,
and you can't control other people.
You can control yourself.

DO SOMETHING

- Help someone else
- Volunteer
- Surprise someone you care about
- Do something thoughtful for someone you don't know

INTENSE SENSATIONS

- Hold ice in hand
- Squeeze ball hard
- Stand in hot/cold shower
- Listen to loud music

SUBSTITUTE THOUGHTS

- Count to 10
- Count colors in a painting or tree
- Watch TV • Think about something else

TRY SOMETHING DIFFERENT

- Listen to emotional music
- Move to a different room or go outside and use your senses (see p. 18 or 36) to notice qualities of this new space

READ

- Read something inspiring
- Read an emotional book
- Read a funny card

GET ACTIVE

- Participate in hobbies
- Exercise • Go for a walk
- Call a friend • Read a book
- Draw • Paint • Listen to music

PROS AND CONS

- Compare yourself to others in tough situations
- Think about the consequences

TAKE A BREAK

- Take a break from the situation
- Don't think about it
- Imagine putting the situation in a box for awhile

SELF-SOOTHE with the 5 SENSES

Things you SEE: watch a funny movie; look at pictures; look at the scenery; look at nature; look at the sunrise/sunset.

What you HEAR: listen to relaxing music; listen to the sounds of nature (wind, birds, rain, rustling leaves); call a friend.

What you SMELL: use your favorite soap; smell good food; bake something; try smelling something in nature (grass, flowers).

Foods you TASTE: really taste what you are eating; try a new food; have a soothing drink like tea or hot chocolate; treat yourself to dessert.

Things you TOUCH: put lotion on; brush your hair; hug someone; hold a basketball/football; hold a book; take a soothing shower.

Return to Center, Time to Reflect

What are the negative ways you reacted in situations that you regret?
Begin to let go of the past. Write a forgiveness letter to yourself and let your burdens be lifted.

Dear Self, I forgive you for...

Return to Center—Back to Our Bodies

"I live in my Truth. I stay centered and let go of the things that no longer serve me."

Resiliency

One way to think about the negative ways you might have reacted in the past is that you were doing the best that you could with what was going on in your life at that time. While in Downward Triangle pose, really let go of who you were to make room for the new you. Open your jaw and even stick out your tongue. Exhale with a "ha" sound, and release any tension in your face. Say to yourself, **"I live in my Truth. I stay centered and let go of the things that no longer serve me."** Feel your feet on the floor rooted in who you are, Imagine anything that you don't want to carry anymore just rolling off your back and shoulders!

Say to yourself,

"I live in my Truth. I stay centered and let go of the things that no longer serve me."

Return to Center—Back to Our Breath

Expanding Awareness of the Breath

Place your hands on the sides of your lower rib cage (above the belly and below the upper chest). Focus your awareness on your breath as it moves in and out of your body through your nose. As you inhale, your belly lifts, your ribs expand, and your chest rises. As you exhale, your chest drops, your ribs contract, and your belly softens and lowers. Continue for up to five minutes, or for as long as you feel comfortable.

Restorative Practice
4-7-8 Breath (Dr. Andrew Weil)

First, let your lips part. Make a whooshing sound, exhaling completely through your mouth.

Next, close your lips, inhaling silently through your nose as you count to four in your head.

Then, for seven seconds, hold your breath.

Make another whooshing exhale from your mouth for eight seconds.

Only practice 4-7-8 breathing for four breaths when you're first starting out. You can gradually work your way up to eight full breaths.

Truthfulness in yoga is being honest with ourselves and others. It is also more than just telling the truth. It is knowing that truth is the deepest wisdom inside ourselves. From that place, we choose our words for the least harm and most good.

TRY THIS **Offer to help one person today.**

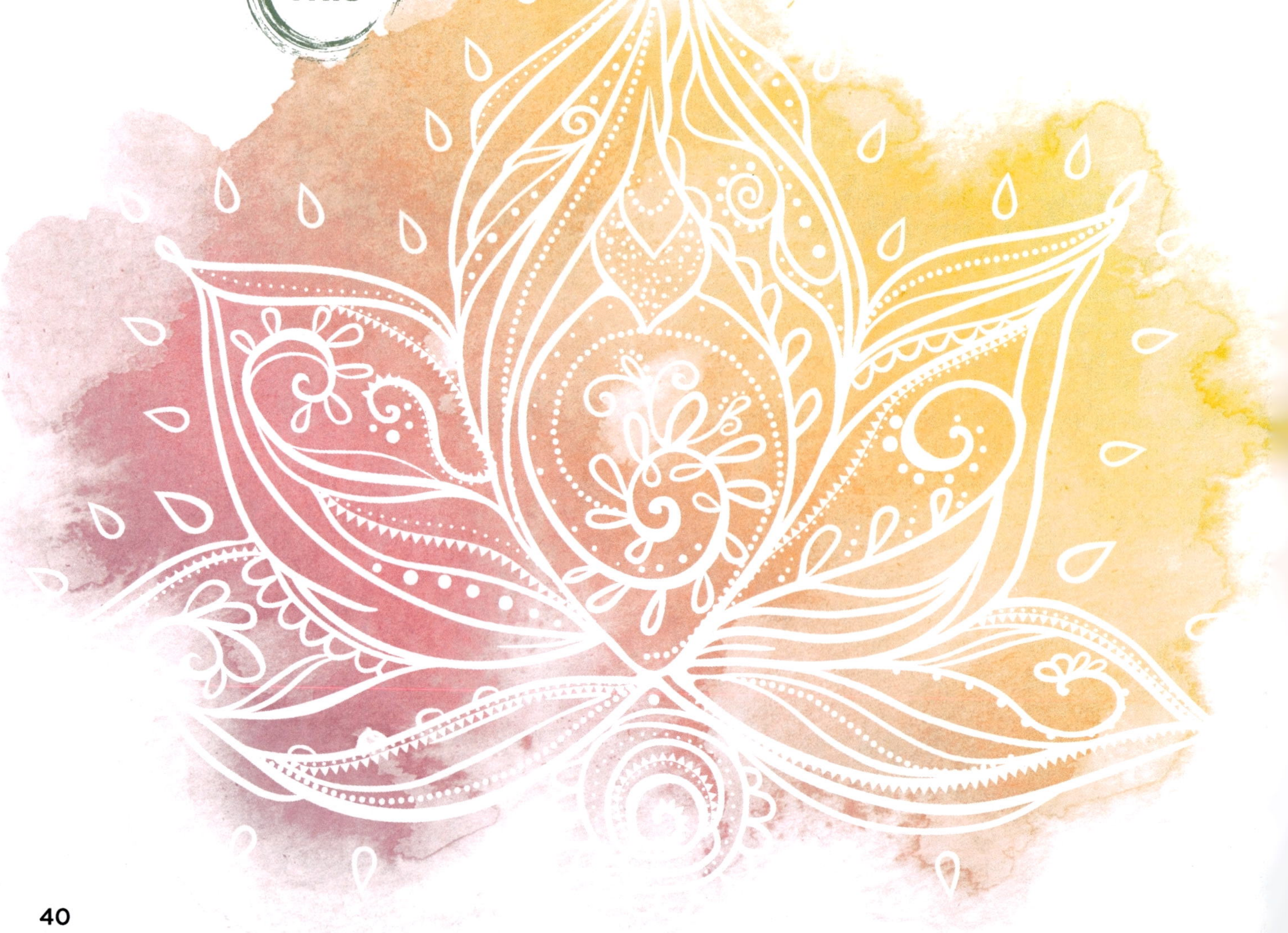

CHAPTER 6

Cultivating Patience

"I am patient and allow my life to unfold."

Sometimes life doesn't feel like it's going our way. We wish things could be different. Maybe people let us down. Maybe we let ourselves down, or maybe we are not able to do the things we want to. It's easy to just stay angry and blame other people or our life circumstances for our problems and negative feelings. Remember that our true power is within us, and we lose our energy through being angry and frustrated. Yoga helps us keep our power by leading us back to our center through the body and breath.

When life is not going the way we want, or other people are not responding the way we want, we can respond in a way that is in alignment with our life values rather than reacting from our emotions.

Let's look at the Skill Sheet "Act, Don't React" on the next page and consider its suggestions for handling conflicts with others in the best way possible and staying focused on what is most in our control: ourselves. We can manage life's challenges by staying balanced and acting in line with our core values. By not reacting, we can continue to cultivate good qualities such as patience, love, forgiveness, and truthfulness in the midst of life's stresses or problems.

When we are ignorant or negative we do not think clearly, and may be impulsive, reckless, and reactive. When we are impatient with ourselves or life's situations, we may react negatively or ignorantly, struggling to control other people or the situation. Patience, on the other hand, helps us to allow things to unfold naturally. When we see things clearly and act with skill and intention, secure in ourselves, we can respect the feelings and opinions of others and surrender to the outcomes of situations.

Think about a flower bud. Can we force the flower to open? No, the flower grows in its own time and its own way. We can only support it with positive conditions—warmth, sunshine, and water—and surrender to what is meant to be.

What are the conditions that you want to put in your life to provide the most growth for you?

Patience and surrender are necessary to let our lives unfold in the best possible way. By going with the flow of life rather than against it, we can stay in our center and let every thought, word, and action be in line with our core values, thus helping us fulfill our life's purpose.

ACT, Don't React

Skills for tough times:

Controlling what is in our control ⟶ OURSELVES

ACT

Assertive, not aggressive

- Be aware of thoughts and feelings.
- Manage your anger.
- Know what you want.

Confident and calm

- Be calm and gentle.
- Come with respect.
- Keep your cool; be understanding.

Try

- Try to think about all the options.
- Try to look at the other person's feelings/side.
- Try negotiating (you need to give to get).
- Tell your feelings using "I" statements.

Describe a situation where you used the ACT skill. How did it go?

____

____

____

____

____

____

____

____

____

Return to Center—Time to Reflect

There are four ways that ignorance and negativity are fed. What are four skillful actions we can do in each of these areas to break free of these negative patterns? For example, to break free from selfishness, I will help someone today without any focus on what's in it for me.

To break free of selfishness, I will____ .

To break free of desire, I will ____ .

To break free of hate, I will____ .

To break free of fear, I will ____ .

Return to Center—Back to Our Bodies

"I release the things that do not serve me. I open myself to positive ways to live my life."

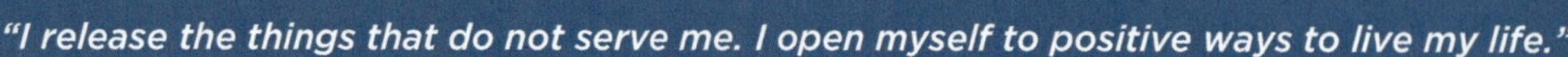

Purification

STANDING FORWARD FOLD

Stand in Mountain Pose, hands on hips. Exhale and bend forward from the hip joints, not from the waist. Bend at the knees if it is easier on your lower back. Bring your palms or finger tips towards the floor slightly in front of or beside your feet. If this isn't possible, cross your forearms and hold your elbows. Release any tension in the back, head, neck, and shoulders. Say to yourself, **"I release the things that do not serve me. I open myself to positive ways to live my life."**

Say to yourself,
"I release the things that do not serve me. I open myself to positive ways to live my life."

Focusing the Mind (or Chin Mudra)

Bringing two fingers together can help you focus your mind and become more aware. Take a comfortable seated position, either on the floor or in a chair. Keeping the jaw relaxed and the spine upright, rest your hands upon your knees or thighs and bring the fingers together by holding the forefinger to the thumb, and extending the other three fingers out. Start to focus the mind by bringing attention to the points where your fingertips touch. Then, move your attention to the breath and begin to move deeper into meditation. You can practice with your palms facing up to encourage receptivity and help gain insight, or it can be practiced with the palms facing down, which encourages a sense of grounding.

Return to Center—Back to Our Breath

Deep Relaxation Breathing

Take a deep breath and exhale. Next try inhaling through your nose for four seconds—count 1, 2, 3, 4. Then exhale through your mouth for six seconds—count 1, 2, 3, 4, 5, 6. Try doing this for two to five minutes.

Restorative Practice

Palming the Eyes

Sit comfortably or lie down. Relax your back and shoulders and exhale out any stress or tension. Rub your hands together vigorously; you may feel a warmth or a tingling sensation. Next, cup your palms and place them over your closed eyes. Your palms are not directly touching the eyes but cupped around the eyes, resting around the eye sockets. Let your fingers relax and rest on your forehead and temples. Don't press on the eye sockets or cheekbones. Let yourself breathe deeply while resting in warmth and peace. Relax and enjoy.

Kindness (or Ahimsa)

Yoga encourages kindness and nonviolence toward all living things—including animals. It means respecting the unity of all living beings and the connection we all share.

Let someone less fortunate than you know that you are thinking of them.

This person may be sick, elderly, or lonely. Maybe give them a phone call, write a letter, or visit, if you can. Send positive thoughts to that person and then send positive thoughts to all people in the world who may be suffering emotionally, physically, financially, or spiritually.

make it happen

CHAPTER 7

The True Purpose of Your Life

"I stay focused on my life purpose and live my life in love and peace."

"Why were you born on this Earth?" Is it just to enjoy pleasures, acquire material things, and die? Or does our human life have a greater value? Think about what you focus on in your life. Do you spend a lot of energy by living your life stuck on issues that focus on yourself, seeking pleasure and power?

When we use our minds, we can live with awareness and turn off the auto pilot, which causes us to react unconsciously from our instincts. When we stop reacting impulsively, we can choose how we want to use our energy and channel it towards our life goals, our life purpose.

How can we live life with a higher purpose? Negative tendencies—such as pride, selfishness, anger, impatience, and greed—can consume and drain our energy, keeping us from developing our full potential. By weakening our negative tendencies, we will have more energy for positive thoughts and actions.

On the next page, you will find the "Reviewing Your Day" Skill Sheet. When we review our day with awareness, we can be more mindful of the skills that we are developing to be more conscious in our actions rather than just reacting. When things get difficult, it's important for us to stay mindful and skillful. Meditation can also help us be more at peace with the challenges in our lives. Living with a higher purpose, we also need to let go of our tendency toward selfishness.

There is a life philosophy in the Native American tradition that encourages us to consider the impact of our actions on the next seven generations. Similarly, in yoga, our practice is not only about helping ourselves, but also about helping others, including our community and the world.

"In our every deliberation, we must consider the impact of our decisions on the next seven generations."

Great Law of the Iroquois

SKILL SHEET

Reviewing Your Day

How did I use my **Diamond** strengths and best qualities today? (Review pg. 12.)

How did I handle my stress today?

Was I able to practice mindfulness in my day?

Did I have a hard time with things or people that were not in my control?

How did I handle it?

Did I practice **Distract** and **Self-Soothe** skills? (Review pgs. 35 and 36.)

Was there a situation where I reacted rather than acted?

What could I have done differently to practice the **ACT** skills? (Review pg. 42.)

Was there a situation when I practiced the **ACT** skills and made myself proud? (Review pg. 42.)

Kindness—Pass It On

Smile at someone • Say, "Hello" • Give a compliment • Help someone
Surprise someone • Give a gift • Share • Encourage a friend
Forgive mistakes • Recycle • Listen to your heart • Be tolerant • Be respectful
Contact someone who is sick • Write a thank you card

Return to Center—Time to Reflect

Ikigai is a Japanese word meaning reason for being. What is the purpose of your life? When you die, what are the things you want to be remembered by? Go back to your "Life Diamond" on page 12 in this workbook. What kind of person do you want to be remembered as?

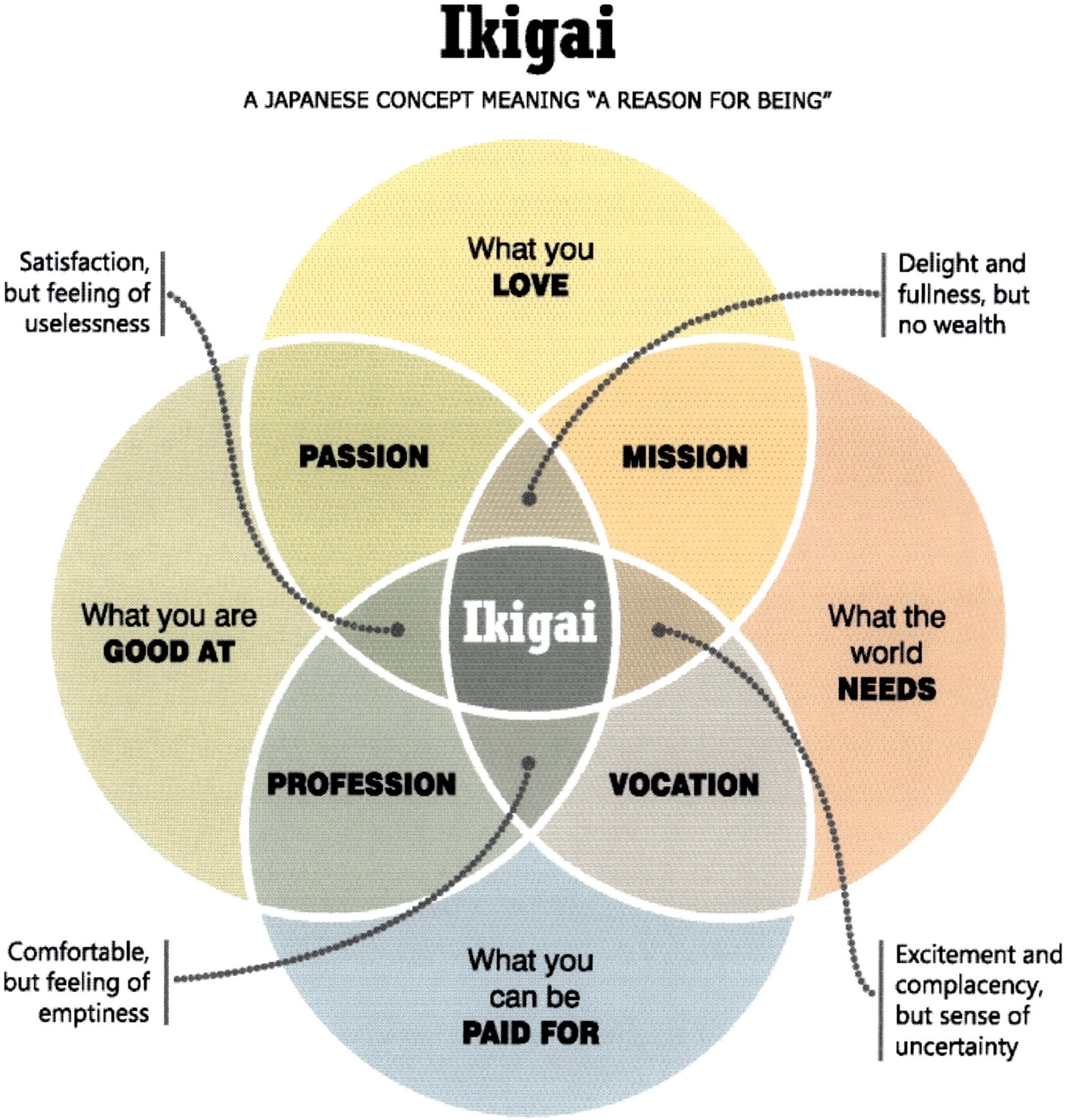

Return to Center—Back to Our Bodies

"I surrender all my burdens in this moment. I am free and at peace."

Closing & Integration

CHILD'S POSE

For Child's Pose, begin by kneeling on the floor. If you can, sit on your heels. If you cannot, it's okay. You can keep your knees and thighs together and put a pillow under your bottom and above your heels for more support. Bring your head down as far as comfortable. Exhale and bring your arms, with palms down, to the floor, bringing the head down as close to the floor as you can without strain. Lengthen your spine and let your head relax towards the floor. Let go completely and say to yourself, **"I surrender all my burdens in this moment. I am free and at peace."** Let yourself rest in this feeling for a while.

Say to yourself,
"I surrender all my burdens in this moment. I am free and at peace."

Return to Center—Back to Our Breath

Breathing to Relieve Stress

Make a soft fist with your hand and gently tap all the parts of your body. Tap your shoulders, neck, face, arms, stomach, back, legs and feet. Now work your way back up the body to the legs, stomach, back, and arms, ending in the middle of your chest with a light tapping. While still tapping the chest, open the jaw and make the "ahhh" sound, exhaling completely. Now make a gentle brushing motion with your hands over all the parts of your body. Imagine brushing away any stress and negativity. Feel renewed and rejuvenated. Know that whenever you are stressed you can take a big inhale, open your jaw, and exhale ahhh to relieve stress.

Restorative Practice

Bumblebee Breath

Sit comfortably or lie down. You can allow your eyes to close, or keep them open if you prefer. Take a few deep breaths to settle in and notice the state of your mind. If you'd like, put your hands over your ears to block out any sound. When you're ready, inhale. Then, for the entire length of your exhalation, make a low-to medium-pitched humming "Mmm" sound in the throat.

Notice how the sound gently vibrates your tongue, teeth, and sinuses. Imagine the sound coming from your heart center (the center of your chest). Do this practice for six rounds of breath. Then, keeping your eyes closed, return to your normal breathing. Notice if anything has changed in how you feel.

Purpose (or Dharma)

When we live our life purpose, we are living in harmony with ourselves and with nature. When we live our life purpose, we are living out our destiny!

TRY THIS

Give away something that means a lot to you, and know that you will be okay without the material item and that you will be gaining something more from helping someone else. Trust that someone else will benefit more from what you are giving away. Feel free.

CHAPTER 8

Love Is the Answer

"I freely give and receive love."

Is the glass half full or half empty? Both answers could be correct, depending on what we choose to focus on in our lives. Do we appreciate what we have or obsess over what we do not have?

Researchers have found that being grateful for what we have has been shown to increase happiness.

It's easy to think about all the things we want or all the things that could make our lives better if only circumstances changed, if only people changed, or if only we had this or didn't have that. But when we stop to appreciate what we do have, remember the true purpose of our life, and make choices in line with that purpose, we can find a greater fulfillment.

Just like we need to mindfully decrease our negative feelings, we also need to mindfully increase our positive feelings. Researchers have found that 10% of our happiness is our external circumstances and 90% is our inner world.

When is the last time you felt happy? Increasing positive feelings is a skill we can use to deal with life's challenges. Using the skill of "Activities You Enjoy" on the next page, you can increase your feelings of happiness and joy, and, in tough times, distract yourself if negative emotions get too intense.

Martin Luther King, Jr. said, "Darkness cannot drive out darkness; only light can do that. Hate cannot drive out hate; only love can do that." Only by bringing in positivity and light can we drive out negativity and darkness.

Think about a glass of salty water. By adding fresh water, we can decrease the taste of the salt. Similarly, in our lives, we can increase the positive ways we think, feel, and act. By this alone, we can gradually lessen the negative.

Think about how we can increase flow in our bodies and minds through balancing opposing energies. We can bring calm when we feel agitated and bring energy when we feel dull. When we are in balance, we have more positive qualities such as compassion, moderation and humility. When we have good soil in a garden, positive things can grow. In yoga, cultivating good qualities in our practice and in our lives can lead the way to not just feeling better in the moment, but to lasting happiness. Temporary pleasures do not last. When we focus on our true purpose in life, we can open our hearts to experience lasting love, peace and happiness.

Activities You Enjoy

1. Planning my career
2. Laughing
3. Reading
4. Having a visit
5. Relaxing
6. Watching a movie
7. Jogging, walking
8. Listening to music
9. Thinking, "I have done a full day's work"
10. Recalling past positive memories
11. Lying in the sun
12. Getting out of (paying on) debt
13. Thinking about my past adventures
14. Listening to others
15. Reading magazines or newspapers
16. Remembering beautiful scenery
17. Meeting new people
18. Saving money
19. Eating
20. Doodling
21. Exercising
22. Cooking
23. Singing
24. Sleeping
25. Having a day with nothing to do
26. Thinking I'm an okay person
27. Doing arts and crafts
28. Writing a letter
29. Making a gift for someone
30. Practicing religion (going to church, group praying, etc.)
31. Writing diary entries or letters
32. Writing books (poems, articles)
33. Doing something new
34. Discussing books

35. Watching TV
36. Making lists of tasks
37. Completing a task
38. Thinking about pleasant events
39. Going hiking
40. Being alone
41. Cleaning
42. Dancing
43. Debating
44. Playing cards
45. Thinking about family
46. Having a political discussion
47. Dressing up and looking nice
48. Reflecting on how you've improved
49. Talking on the phone
50. Thinking positive thoughts
51. Listening to the radio
52. Saying "I love you"
53. Thinking about your good qualities
54. Fantasizing about the future
55. Having lunch with a friend
56. Thinking about becoming active in the community
57. Collecting things (positive articles, inspirational quotes, etc.)
58. Making jigsaw puzzles
59. Thinking I'm a person who can cope
60. ______________________________

Return to Center—Time to Reflect

Look at your life as "half full" rather than "half empty." What are all the things that you are grateful for? What are all the things you appreciate?

Gratitude

I am grateful for...

Return to Center—Back to Our Bodies

"In this moment, I let go of my stress and tension and, with every breath, fill with more peace and happiness."

Centering & Opening

Lie on the floor. Bend your knees and set your feet on the floor, heels as close to your hips as possible. Exhale, and pressing your inner feet and arms actively into the floor, lift your hips off the floor. Keep your thighs and inner feet parallel. Clasp your hands below your hips and extend through your arms to help you stay on the tops of your shoulders. Lengthen your spine and breathe. Lift your chin slightly away from your chest, and bringing your shoulder blades against your back, press the top of your chest toward your chin. Breathe and say to yourself, **"In this moment, I let go of my stress and tension and, with every breath, fill with more peace and happiness."**

Say to yourself,
"In this moment, I let go of my stress and tension and, with every breath, fill with more peace and happiness."

Return to Center—Back to Our Breath

Alternate Nostril Breathing

Sit comfortably, cross-legged, if you are able. Using the left thumb, softly close the left nostril and inhale as slowly as you can through the right nostril, and then close it with your ring finger. Pause. Open and exhale slowly through the left nostril. With the left nostril open, inhale slowly, and then close it with your thumb. Pause. Exhale through the right nostril. Once your exhalation is complete, inhale through the right. Pause before moving to the left. Repeat this pattern five to ten times, and then release the left hand to the left knee. Let yourself return to normal breathing.

take a deep breath

- Inhale Right
- Close & Hold
- Exhale Left
- Inhale Left
- Close & Hold
- Exhale Right

Restorative Practice
Legs up the Wall

LEGS UP WALL

Find an open wall space or use a chair or bed to comfortably put your feet up. Start seated on the floor beside the wall, chair, or bed. On an exhale, gently lie down on your back and pivot yourself so that the backs of your legs are pressing against the wall and the bottoms of your feet are facing up.

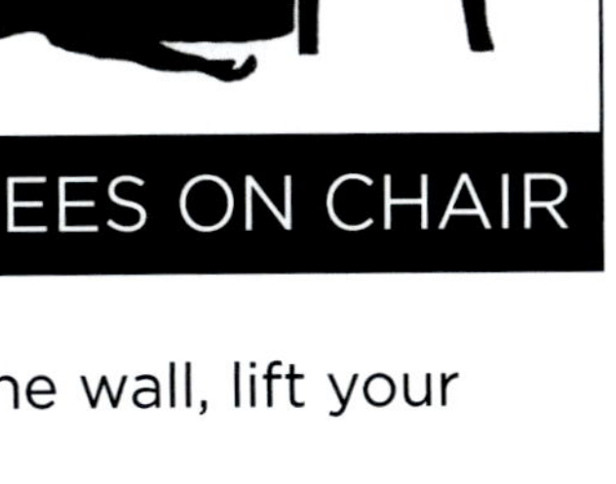

KNEES ON CHAIR

If you are using a chair or bed, your knees are bent, allowing the calves and feet to be relaxed. Your back, hands, and head are resting on the floor. If you find this position uncomfortable in any way on the wall, or just wish for extra cushion, you can use your pillow or a block. (By pressing the bottoms of your feet into the wall, lift your hips slightly and slide your pillow or block underneath your hips.)

Let the back of your head be heavy and your neck be in a neutral position. Soften your face and your throat. Let your hands rest either on your belly or down by your sides, palms facing upward. If you feel comfortable, close your eyes or just keep them open if you prefer. Breathe deeply through your nose. Stay here for anywhere from 5–15 minutes.

To come out of the position, push the bottoms of your feet into the wall and lift your hips slightly. Gently roll to one side, being sure to slide your support out of the way if you have used one. Stay on your side for a few breaths before returning to your seated position. Notice how you feel.

Sound Meditation

People from every religious tradition practice some form of meditation, filling their minds with awareness of the sacred as they understand it.

Sound creates vibrations within us that can calm our minds and create more peace in our hearts. This Ma-Om meditation technique was given by a great humanitarian Sri Mata Amritanandamayi Devi (known to millions simply as 'Amma'). Thousands of people around the world have practiced it and have experienced its peace. You can do it too. It is very easy.

When people start to meditate, it is recommended that they try to do it at the same time and in the same place every day. Don't get worry or be tense about this. Just be willing to do your best one day at a time. Choose a place that is clean, quiet and safe. Choose a time when you can be undisturbed for some time. If you are not able to do this one day, it's okay. Just try again the next day.

Circle of Love Inside is Amma's prison outreach letter-writing program. If you would like to receive letters or learn more information please contact: Circle of Love Inside, P.O. Box 613, San Ramon, CA 94583.

1. Sit comfortably with your back straight. Close your eyes, if you feel comfortable doing so. Otherwise, look downward.

2. Chant the sound om three times either out loud or mentally.

3. Think of whatever cultivates love within your heart. It can be whatever image, name, or form of God that resonates with you or simply qualities, such as peace and love, within your own heart. Or, think of a divine light that radiates love and light within your heart.

4. Watch your breathing. Don't try to breathe in any special way. Just pay attention to your breathing. Notice how the inhalation and exhalation feels.

5. Hear the sound "ma" when you inhale and "om" when you exhale. Continue this for some time. Maaa...Ommm... Maaa...Ommm... Maaa...Ommm... Maaa...Ommm... Maaa...Ommm... Maaa...Ommm... As you do this, imagine breathing in divine love when you inhale Maaa and breathing out divine light on the Ommm. Your attention naturally shifts from breathing to experiencing divine love and light. Maaa... Ommm... Maaa...Ommm... As you continue, you will become more and more still. Let yourself feel deep love and inner peace.

6. Now, let the thought of Ma and Om go. Let it vanish into profound peace, sweet joy, and silence. Let your mind be as open and expansive as the sky. Imagine this love and peace filling your entire being and then spreading out to all beings in the world.

7. Say this chant for peace three times in either English or Sanskrit: English: May all beings everywhere be happy and peaceful. Sanskrit: Lokah samastah sukhino bhavantu Om Shanti, Shanti, Shanti-hi (three times).

Yoga cultivates a state of unconditional love or self-compassion for ourselves and also compassion for others. It is a love that is full and awakens the wisdom within us.

Compliment one person today.

CHAPTER 9

We Need Each Other

"I always see the good in others and live with others in love and peace."

Throughout this program we have learned that we need to look inside ourselves for true happiness. When we feel content and have self-love for who we are, we cannot help but want the best for others. What happens to a cup when it's full? When we fill up our own hearts with love and peace we are overflowing and want others to experience these feelings as well. Certain meditations can help us to be accepting and kind not only to ourselves, but also to others whom we may like or dislike.

By living in harmony with others, we can achieve so much more. Researchers have found that geese flying together in a V formation add 71% more flying power than when flying alone!

Although we might have differences, we also have a sameness underneath. Remember the word namaste, which means "the light in me honors the light in you." We all have the same light—that precious human spirit—within us. We all have breath as our life energy. How different, then, can we be from each other? Yoga helps us stay grounded in who we are and what we have in common with others. The deeper we can rest in this understanding, the more peace we will experience within ourselves. When we are in conflict with others (e.g., when we are in an argument) it's hard to remember this deeper understanding. The "MINDFUL" Skill on the next page can help us to not react from our emotions but, instead, maintain the relationship while sticking to our core values. If you feel like your emotions are too overwhelming to practice the MINDFUL skill, try the "MEANING" skill on the following page first, to help you take a break and ride the wave of emotion, and then to be able to work out the situation in a more positive way.

MINDFUL Skill

Mindful: Stay focused on your topic. Breathe.

Interested: Be gentle and easy, smile, and use humor.

Negotiate: Stick to your values, but you might have to give some to get some.

Describe: Use facts; don't lie. Acknowledge the other person's feelings and own your opinions.

Fair: Be fair to yourself and to others.

Use Assertiveness: Be confident with voice, tone, and manner.

Listen: Listen to the other person, be interested, and listen to what your values are.

MEANING Skill

Create meaningful moments

When practicing this skill, we are not trying to CHANGE the external circumstance, but rather trying to improve the moment to make it more tolerable (even more enjoyable) for just this moment. Remember, thoughts and emotions come and go like ocean waves.

Meaningful: Find or create some purpose, meaning, or value in the pain. Focus on any positive aspects that you can find in the painful situation.

Encourage yourself: Cheer yourself on. Repeat over and over, "I can stand it," "It won't last forever," "I will make it out of this," "I am doing the best I can do."

Attention: Focus your entire attention on what you are doing right now. Keep yourself in the moment you are in. Put your mind in the present.

No tension: Try relaxing and tensing each large muscle, take a hot shower, breathe deeply, half smile, change your facial expression.

Imagine: Imagine very relaxing scenes. Imagine everything going well. Imagine coping well...

New perspective: Open your heart to a supreme being, greater wisdom, God, or your own wise mind. Ask for strength to bear the pain in the moment.

Go on vacation: Take a brief trip. If you can't get away from the situation, find a way to take a break. Read something interesting, have a snack, or go to bed. Enjoy your break.

Return to Center—Time to Reflect

Centering Practice

This program encourages us to look at prayer from a universal perspective. A great humanitarian, Amma (Mata Amritanandamayi) shared that whenever she is asked about her religion, she replies that her religion is love. She does not ask anyone to believe in God or to change their faith, only to go deeper into their faith, to inquire into their own real nature and to believe in themselves. Think of a sacred word that will remind you of this deep truth within you.

What is your sacred word? ________________________________

In what situations or places could you use your sacred word to help you stay centered?

____

____

____

____

____

____

Return to Center—Back to Our Bodies

"I meet life's challenges with patience, courage, and balance."

Purification

Inhale and lift your torso with your shoulders directly over your wrists. Firm your shoulder blades against your back, then spread them away from your spine. Also spread your collarbones away from your sternum. Look straight down at the floor, releasing the base of your neck and keeping your throat and eyes soft. Feel your strength and balance. Say to yourself, **"I meet life's challenges with patience, courage, and balance."**

Say to yourself,

"I meet life's challenges with patience, courage, and balance."

Return to Center—Back to Our Breath

Meditation Stopping the War Within

Let yourself sit comfortably and breathe normally. Let your attention be on the present moment. Let go of thoughts about the past or future. Let yourself be full here now.

Notice any sensations that you feel in your body. Do you feel any muscle tensions or pain? Try not to change them, just notice them and bring kindness to them. Let go of the struggle to make them go away and just be present with them and let your body relax and your heart soften.

Now turn your attention to any inner wars you have been fighting—your own anger, loneliness, fear or addictions. Again, simply notice these emotions with kind attention and let your heart and mind soften. Let go of the inner struggle and just be present and open with compassionate attention to yourself letting all the parts of yourself be at peace.

Return to Center—Back to Our Breath

Restorative Practice
Healing Light Meditation

Stress can play a large part in many health problems such as headaches, high blood pressure, heart problems, diabetes, sleep problems, depression, and anxiety. Of all doctor's office visits, 75% to 90% are for stress-related issues. When we can let go of stress in our bodies through yoga and meditation, it gives the body a chance to heal itself. This healing light meditation gives an opportunity for the body to let go of stored stress, calming the mind and allowing the body an opportunity to self-heal. It is not necessary to actually "see" the light when you are asked to visualize it during this exercise. To simply feel that the light is present is enough.

Let yourself sit or lie down comfortably. Just notice the inhalation and exhalation of your breath. Visualize the most beautiful light you have ever seen. It can be whatever color you would like. Imagine this divine light shining brighter than the Sun within your heart center.

As you are noticing your breath flowing in and out, imagine the light getting brighter and brighter. On the inhalation and exhalation, imagine this light accompanied with a feeling of love and compassion for you. Now let this divine light and love spread throughout your whole body bringing warm, healing energy to all your body parts. This light is filling you with warmth and love, moving to your feet... to your legs... to your torso... to your hips... to your lower back... to your stomach... to your upper back... to your chest... to your shoulders... to your arms... to your hands... to your neck... to your head... to your jaw... to your eyes... to your face. Let this healing light, love and warmth spread throughout your entire body. Let your breath bring that healing energy to every particle of blood, every cell, every tissue, and every organ. Let this radiant energy cleanse your innermost being, cleansing you physically, emotionally, mentally, and spiritually.

Now this healing energy grows and expands. Allow yourself to see, feel, and sense this energy surrounding your entire being, growing and growing. Allow this energy to spread throughout the room... the building... out into nature... to the oceans... the mountains... the animals...and, finally, throughout the entire universe, reaching, touching, and blessing all. Imagine this divine light and love circling back into your own heart center, nourishing your whole being with revitalizing new energy. Let yourself relax in this feeling of peace and calm throughout your body and mind.

Youth Testimonials

Take a minute and notice if anything has shifted in your life since you started practicing yoga. How does your body feel? How do you manage your thoughts? How do you cope with your emotions? What in your life is better? Here are some words from our youth. Please feel free to share with us how things are going for you (our mailing address is on pg. 83)!

"I feel like I can make better decisions now. I feel empowered."

"Yoga helps me with my anger. It helps me calm down, relax and take my mind off stuff. I told my momma about it. Now she has tried deep breathing and it has helped her. I told her we will do yoga together when I get out."

"Yoga helps me relieve my stress. I can catch myself getting stressed and do yoga things throughout the day like take a deep breath and rotate my shoulders, and it will help me relax. It helps me take the stress off."

"Yoga helps me calm down and focus on what's important and what's not important. For example, rather than focusing on all the time I have to do, I can look at all the opportunities I've been given. Rather than focus on the negatives, now I can focus on the positives."

"Yoga helps me get away from everything… stress, anger, anxiety… and be in my own world. I feel relaxed and peaceful, and it takes my mind to a different planet."

"I have impulse control problems. Yoga helps me release my anger and stress so I can think before I act. When I got denied my early release, instead of flipping the unit, I took a deep breath. Yoga helped me stop and see the bigger picture and that I can still do good."

"Yoga helps me calm down and relax my mind. It makes me calm and when I think about doing something negative, it makes me feel better about myself and make a better decision."

"Yoga helps me relax and focus. I can tune everything out and relieve stress and think about my life. And it's good exercise too."

"Yoga helps me when I'm not in a good mood."

"I never felt so relaxed and peaceful… I feel so centered and calm."

"Usually in the mornings, I wake up grumpy, but today I feel so good."

Community (or Satsang)

In yoga we try to surround ourselves with positive people and things. When we keep company with others in positive ways, it helps calm our minds and open our hearts.

TRY THIS

Offer to help someone today without thinking about what's in it for you.

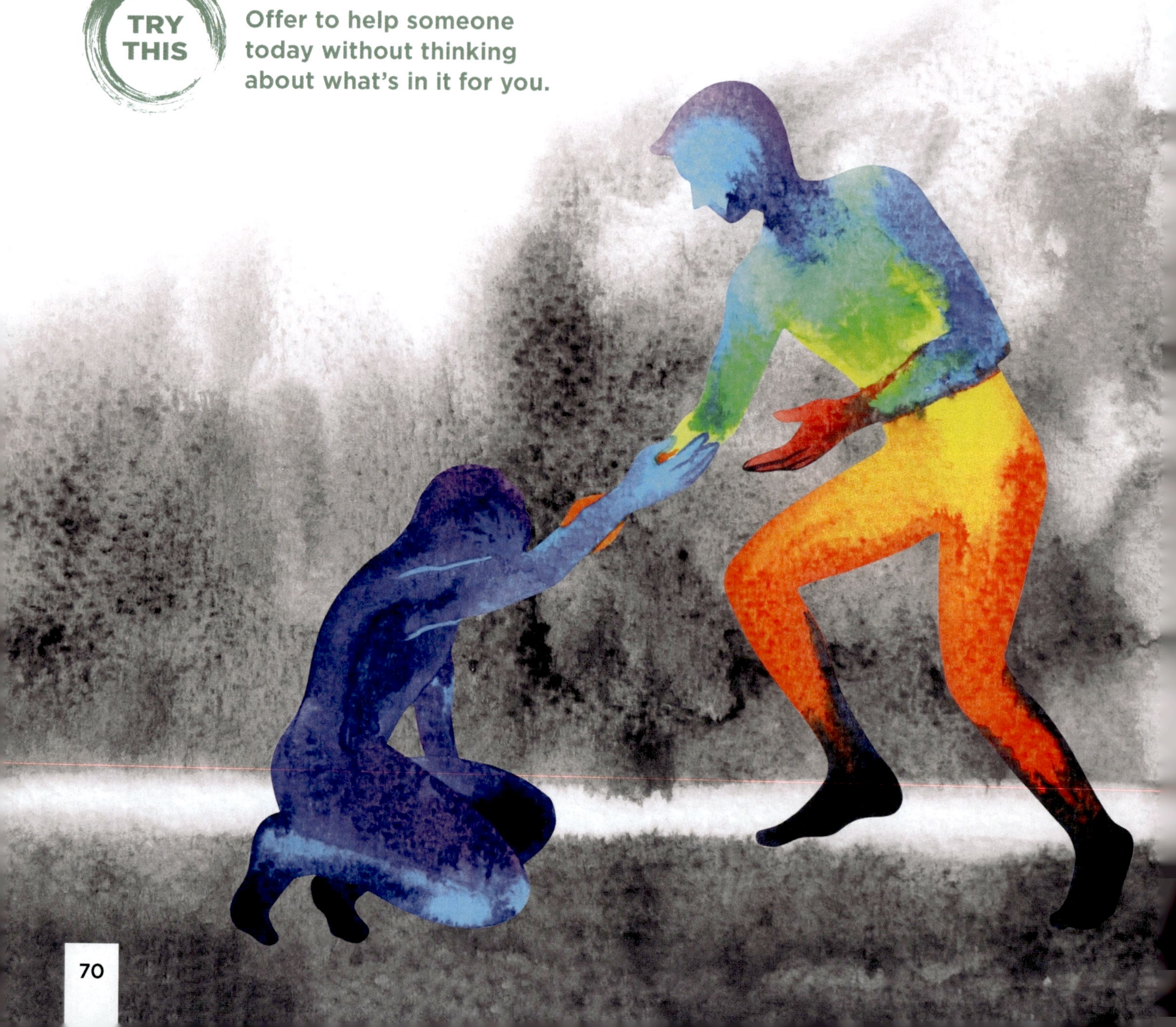

CHAPTER 10

Yoga off the Mat

"I commit to living my life, every day, in love and peace. I choose happiness."

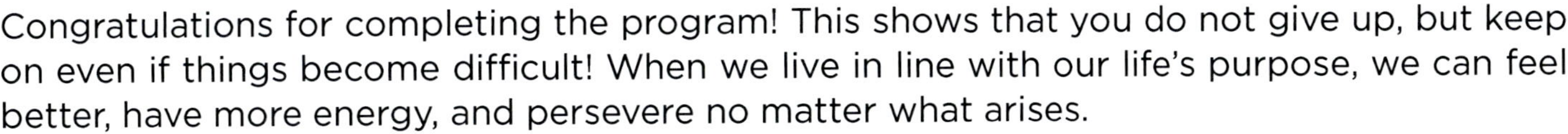

Congratulations for completing the program! This shows that you do not give up, but keep on even if things become difficult! When we live in line with our life's purpose, we can feel better, have more energy, and persevere no matter what arises.

Imagine that you haven't eaten all day, and now you have the choice to eat a candy bar or a regular meal with vegetables and fruits. If you eat the candy bar, it may taste good but the energy that you get will only be temporary. After a short time, you will become hungry and tired again, maybe even more tired than when you started. If you eat a meal instead, you will have lasting energy and not feel hungry as quickly. At first, eating the meal may not be as exciting as eating the candy bar, but in the long run, you know you will have more energy.

Go back and take a look at your "Life Diamond" on page 12. What were some of the things that prevented you from shining? When we look at those poor choices and negative behaviors, they may have made us feel good temporarily and given us short-term relief, but in the long term, they caused us more problems.

What allows us to stay peaceful when things get difficult? Yoga is like making a tent in the middle of a hurricane. Life may bring storms and strong winds, but we can stay centered, protected, and secure in our tent within.

Yoga can help us stay calm and clear when life tries to stress us out. The more we practice yoga, the more we can stay focused on the bigger picture and participate in decision-making processes that give us long-term peace and happiness—not just temporary pleasures or relief.

Return to Center—Time to Reflect

Our greatest resource is who we are and how we choose to live life. Children were asked what they appreciated most from their parents, and it wasn't what their parents had bought them. Instead, what was truly cherished was the time they had spent and the positive memories they shared together. How do children spell love? For children, L-O-V-E is spelled T-I-M-E.

We should use our time, energy, and resources wisely to make all activities in service of our core values, and life's purpose and goals.

One way to help us live in line with our core values is to determine what we truly need and what is extra. If we are not mindful in our daily pursuits, we will never discover lasting peace and joy. Instead, we will continue to waste our precious time and energy, suffering further frustration and fatigue.

Yoga "off the mat" involves mindful awareness of every thought, word, and action to make sure it is in service of our higher good.

Ghandi said,
"Your beliefs become your thoughts,
Your thoughts become your words,
Your words become your actions,
Your actions become your habits,
Your habits become your values,
Your values become your destiny."

Reviewing our day *mindfully* can help us achieve our life's destination.

Return to Center—Back to Our Bodies

"I let go and trust the process of life. I have faith."

Closing & Integration

BODY TWIST

Relax on your back and bring both knees up, with your feet flat on the floor. Your feet should be hip-width apart. Bring your arms out like a T. Gently lower your knees to the left side of your body and place them on the floor. Gaze right and breathe. Say to yourself, "I let go and trust the process of life. I have faith." Engage your abdominals and slowly pull your knees back to the start position. Gently lower your knees to the right side of your body and place them on the floor. Continue breathing while you feel your body and mind letting go into the pose. Again, say to yourself, **"I let go and trust the process of life. I have faith."**

Say to yourself,

"I let go and trust the process of life. I have faith."

Return to Center—Back to Our Breath

"I let go of what does not serve my highest Self and open myself to joy."

Walking Meditation

Take a few deep breaths. Begin walking very slowly. Notice how the ground feels under each foot and how the pressure of your weight shifts from the heel to the ball of the foot. Pay attention to any other sensations in the feet as you walk slowly.

Try "Breath of Joy" to energize and uplift you.

Stand with your feet shoulder-width apart and parallel, knees slightly bent.

1. Inhale one-third of your lung capacity and swing your arms up in front of your body, bringing them parallel to each other at shoulder level, with palms facing the ceiling.

Front Inhale

2. Continue inhaling to two-thirds capacity and stretch your arms out to the side, like wings, to shoulder level.

Side Inhale

3. Inhale to full capacity and swing your arms parallel and over your head, palms facing each other.

Up Inhale

4. Open your mouth and exhale completely with an audible ha, bending the knees more deeply as you sink into a standing squat and swing your arms down and back behind you like a diver.

Exhale "ha"

Repeat up to nine times. Don't force or strain the body or breath. Simply be absorbed by the peacefully stimulating rhythm. Return to standing and say to yourself, **"I let go of what does not serve my highest Self and open myself to joy."** Close your eyes and experience the effects. Notice how quickly your heart beats; feel the sensations in your face and arms, and the tingling in the palms of your hands. Again repeat to yourself, ***"I let go of what does not serve my highest Self and open myself to joy."***

Finding Peace

Dealing with Grief and Loss

Sometimes, when we lose a loved one, the pain can feel unbearable. It might feel like we can't go on.

Author and Nobel Peace Prize-nominated peace activist Thich Nhat Hanh gives us a better understanding of how not to be so sad when we feel that life will never be the same.

"It's like a cloud in the sky. When the cloud is no longer in the sky, it doesn't mean the cloud has died. The cloud is continued in other forms like rain or snow or ice. So you can recognize your cloud in her new forms. If you are very fond of a beautiful cloud and if your cloud is no longer there, you should not be sad. Your beloved cloud might have become the rain, calling on you, 'Darling, darling, don't you see me in my new form?' And then you will not be stuck with grief and despair. Your beloved one continues always. Meditation helps you recognize his continued presence in new forms... You look into the sky and you see a beautiful cloud. The cloud has become the rain. And when you drink your tea, you can see your cloud in your tea."

Restorative Practice
Calming Touch

Start by rubbing your palms together. Next, bring them about an inch apart and notice what you feel between your hands. It may be tingling or warmth. This is your own healing energy. Place your hand anywhere on your body that feels calming and soothing. Try holding both your cheeks with the palms of your hands. Try placing both hands on the center of your chest. Try your forehead, your stomach, over your eyes, anywhere that needs soothing, healing energy. Relax into the warmth of your hands and take in the gentle care through your touch. Breathe into this feeling of comfort and peace.

Reviewing Our Life Values

Planting Positive Seeds in Ourselves and the World

It can be helpful to reexamine our personal value system and look at how we want to live our life. With our core life values as our foundation, we can develop a solid set of principles or ideals that guides and drives what we do. We feel good about doing positive things in line with our values, and they not only help ourselves but others. Here is our Yoga "To Do" list!

Peace in the World

Nonviolence
Don't be violent to myself, others or the environment; be caring in my thoughts and words and avoid any that may injure myself or others.

Truthfulness
Don't lie or deceive; be truthful in my thoughts, words and actions with myself and others.

Non-Stealing
Don't steal or take what is not given; be generous.

Non-indulging
Don't waste my energy; use my energy wisely and with purpose.

Non-possessiveness
Don't be greedy or focus on getting things that are not essential; be grateful for what I have.

Peace with Yourself

Cleanliness
Be clean on both the inside (avoiding anger, ego) and the outside (my body and my environment).

Contentment
Be happy and content with myself and others.

Self-discipline
Always be disciplined and work hard.

Self-study
Studying is important. Take time to learn about myself and the world around me.

Surrender
Always trust the power inside of me and be humble.

Talk the Talk, Walk the Walk

Daily Reflection

Here are some questions to help us reflect and be more intentional each day.

1. What is my ultimate life goal?
2. What is the immediate goal to be realized in order to achieve my ultimate life goal?
3. What effort did I put forth to materialize my ultimate life goal?
4. What effort did I put forth to materialize my immediate goal?
5. What good deed did I do to help others?
6. Did I receive any help from others?
7. What did I do for my own good without regard to my likes or comforts?
8. What did I do to tend to my physical self? How did I tend to my diet/eating? What types of physical exercise did I engage in?
9. What did I do to tend to my emotional self? Did I conquer negative qualities like anger, laziness, despair, envy, hatred and anxiety and nurture positive qualities like joy, contentment, enthusiasm, humility, attention and awareness?
10. What did I do to tend to my intellectual self? What positive things did I study memorize, write, or contemplate?
11. Was I compassionate today? Did my compassion include heartfelt wishes for the removal of pain or sorrow from someone who is neither related to me nor is my friend?
12. Did I scorn, speak ill of or complain about anyone or any situation?
13. Did I console or cheer anyone?

14. What happened today that will be worth recollecting, even after many years? Or what was the most interesting event of the day? Did I hear, read or experience anything funny, wise, thought-provoking, poignant, and/or poetic?
15. Did I spend any time without thought (silent mind, meditating/relaxing, sitting in, or visualizing nature)?

16. What worry is currently dominating my mind? If my best friend were facing this problem, how would I comfort him/her? Is it something that may happen in the future or something that has already happened? If so, is there any use in worrying about it? Can I change it through self-effort and using my skills? Is it a petty issue?
17. Did any of the day's failures or tragedies provide me with a deeper insight into life?
18. Did I commit any mistake today? What did I do today to correct it? What have I done to ensure that it will not be repeated?
19. Did I share with anyone any of my abilities, knowledge or resources in some way?
20. Was I punctual? Did I fulfill my commitments? Did I waste time?
21. Was I able to keep my mind happy and peaceful under all circumstances? Was I able to talk to everyone with a smile?
22. Did I take anything extra from nature or society, or did I waste anything (like water, electricity, food, or fuel)? Did I recycle any resources I could have?
23. Was I able to not overindulge with food? While eating, was I able to maintain an attitude of gratitude?
24. Did I set aside some time to maintain silence or be fully aware of each thought, word, breath, and action? Did I engage in all activities with mindfulness?

Adapted from: Reflection Diary, Br. Sivamrita Chaitanya, Matruvani March 2009, Vol. X No. 3, p. 24–28.

Every Day is a Fresh Start!

Further Reading

James' book is available free of charge to anyone who is incarcerated. Requests can be made to the address on page 83.

Use the chart below to find exercises and further reading from James Fox's book ***Yoga: A Path for Healing and Recovery*** to deepen your practice.

	The Power of Peace Within Me	Yoga: A Path for Healing and Recovery
CHAPTER 1	Page #	Page #
Real Power Is Within You	5	1
Conscious Breathing	9	6
CHAPTER 2		
Choosing Happiness	11	4
Warrior 1 Pose	14	17
Daily Meditation Practice	15	88
CHAPTER 3		
Go with the Flow of Life	17	76
Lying Down Pose	20	19
Yogic Breathing	21	79
CHAPTER 4		
Being in the Present Moment	23	11
Cat-Cow Pose	26	25
CHAPTER 5		
Letting Go of Negativity	33	22
Self-Forgiveness	37	98
Downward Triangle Pose	38	25
Expanding Awareness of the Breath	39	78
CHAPTER 6		
Cultivating Patience	41	52
Standing Forward Fold Pose	44	25
Deep Relaxation Breathing	45	80
CHAPTER 7		
The True Purpose of Your Life	47	36
Child's Pose	50	13
Breathing to Relieve Stress	51	81
CHAPTER 8		
Love Is the Answer	53	53
Bridge Pose	56	55
Alternate Nostril Breathing	57	82
CHAPTER 9		
We Need Each Other	61	96
Centering Practice	64	90
Plank Pose	65	29
Meditation Stopping the War Within	66	95
CHAPTER 10		
Yoga off the Mat	71	87
Body Twist Pose	73	69
Walking Meditation	74	92
Reviewing Our Life Values	76	7

Focus, **L**et Go, **A**nger Management, **M**indfulness, **E**xhale Negativity

Our yoga students named themselves, "YOGA FLAME!" We created five skill building yoga sessions that focus on a specific topic for that class. Each class we would watch a YouTube video and practice a yoga sequence from James' book. The sequences were chosen as exercises that focus on using body and breath awareness for that topic. Our research found an average of a 38% reduction in stress with each class!* The sequences can be found in James Fox's book Yoga: A Path for Healing and Recovery, follow the page numbers. If you have access to the internet check out the free videos on YouTube. If not, you can read the description and hopefully when you are able you can check them out.

Focus

Simple Practice: pgs. 20-21

Increase Attention and Concentration

Train Your Mind With LeBron James:
https://www.youtube.com/watch?v=q7rzz9asT7Q

Calm is teaming up with LeBron James to raise awareness about the importance of mental fitness. LeBron credits meditation, sleep, and a healthy mindset as the keys to his extraordinary achievements and personal happiness.

LeBron's "Meditation" During The Time Out:
https://www.youtube.com/watch?v=SCR7OfRuQd4

Check out LeBron James, who has logged heavy minutes throughout the series and in game 7, resting during the timeout and attempting to regain his strength on his way to another huge game, lifting the Heat to the NBA Finals where they will play Kevin Durant and the Oklahoma City Thunder!

Juquille's Story-LIFE Camp
https://www.youtube.com/watch?v=Gdfu54PQLJw

What happens when yoga goes to work in the lives of young people living in neighborhoods known for severe violence? The premiere episode of URBAN YOGIS documents just how powerful the practice can be on people like Juquille Johnston, who lives in a housing project in South Jamaica Queens, New York. Recognized for his talents as a musician and athlete, Juquille has dealt with tremendous hurdles including the loss of his father due to gun violence. Yoga teacher Eddie Stern shows these teenagers how to slow down, breathe, and find peace in the face of enormous challenges.

Let Go

Breath Exercises: pgs. 77-83

Increase Relaxation

Kobe Bryant: The Power of Sleep and Meditation:
https://www.youtube.com/watch?v=LdrVVJPlUK4

Kobe Bryant was always more than a legendary basketball player. Here, Bryant, who felt strongly that well-being is critical for peak performance, shares how prioritizing sleep and meditation benefited his game.

*Eyman, K. (2021). The Effects of Yoga On Incarcerated Youth. Master's Thesis, Cleveland State University. Ohiolink.

Anger Management

Basic Practice: pgs. 34-35

Decrease Aggression

The Horizon Story: Yoga in a Juvenile Detention Facility
https://www.youtube.com/watch?v=BXcO3SSr_vs&list=PLdrUeeBIMbrKiDzK_NTPBH_taIKaEIv3z&index=8&t=0s

Yoga instructor Eddie Stern joins Leslie Booker to teach yoga to teenagers in a juvenile detention facility in the Bronx. Leslie is a teacher with The Lineage Project, an organization that places yoga and meditation instructors in detention centers, public schools, and other community sites around New York. Their mission is to share these practices with youth who might fall victim to crime and violence, in the hope that the healing, grounding tools gained through meditation will help them improve their situations. Hear what the kids have to say about their experience learning yoga!

Mindfulness

Intermediate Practice: pgs. 48-49

Increase Tolerance to Stress and Decrease Impulsivity

Anthony's Story: Yoga and Foster Care
https://www.youtube.com/watch?v=mWd3wXulwRY&list=PLdrUeeBIMbrKiDzK_NTPBH_taIKaEIv3z&index=11

Can a person survive a very difficult childhood and come to truly thrive as an adult? What role might yoga play in this? Anthony grew up in and out of foster care homes, uncertain of the future that lay ahead. Now as an independent college student there is much to be proud of and much to look forward to. Anthony makes yoga a part of his weekly practice, knowing the benefit it has on his mood and ability to focus. Watch what he has to say about his long-term goals and the path forward that he envisions!

Exhale Negativity

Warrior Practice: pgs. 70-73

Increase Emotion Regulation

The RAPP Story: Teens, Domestic Violence, and Yoga
https://www.youtube.com/watch?v=__leoH5ybCM&list=PLdrUeeBIMbrKiDzK_NTPBH_taIKaEIv3z&index=10

The teens in NYC's Relationship Abuse Prevention Program (RAPP) come from homes where they've witnessed violence or been victims of abuse themselves. For one hour a week they visit Eddie Stern's Yoga studio to practice yoga and find peace. As Eddie says, give a teenager ten minutes to lay down and do nothing and they love you. Discover how these teens allow their one hour a week with Eddie to find relaxation and center themselves to better deal with stressful situations.

More about Urban Yogis who created many of the videos above:
URBAN YOGIS is a unique documentary series featuring stories on the transformative power of yoga and meditation. Beautifully shot, inspiring, and heartfelt - the series delves into the lives of cancer survivors, inner-city youth dealing with violence in their communities, recovering addicts, artists, youth in detention facilities, and more. Comedian Russell Brand, Grammy-nominated musician Moby, "yogi" businessman Russell Simmons, and author/doctor Deepak Chopra also share their stories and insights. Renowned yoga teacher Eddie Stern serves as our host and guide to the stories of these urban yogis.

Top 10 Benefits of Yoga

How are you feeling? Yoga has been scientifically proven to have many benefits for our mind-body system. We interviewed youth in our programs and these are the top 10 issues that they felt yoga helped them with the most!

1. **Can't sleep? Try Calming Touch on page 75.** Participants who have practiced yoga have reported a greater ability to fall asleep faster, sleep longer and feel more rested in the mornings.

2. **Stressed out? Try Legs up the Wall on page 57.** Yoga has been shown to ease stress and lower levels of the stress hormone, cortisol.

3. **Headaches? Try Palming the Eyes on page 45.** Yoga can promote a feeling of relaxation and reduce migraines.

4. **Feeling down? Try Hand Over the Heart on page 15.** Practicing yoga can improve quality of life as well as mood and fatigue.

5. **Can't focus? Try Breath Awareness on page 9.** Yoga has been shown to help reduce distracting thoughts and improve concentration and memory.

6. **Angry? Try 4-7-8 Breath on page 39.** Yoga encourages mindfulness and reduces tension in the body so we can better cope with difficult feelings.

7. **Feel tired? Try Breath of Joy on page 74.** Yoga can help boost energy, strength and endurance.

8. **Feel unhealthy? Try Healing Light Meditation on page 67.** Yoga can boost immunity and reduce blood pressure in the body which can lead to diseases like heart disease, diabetes, and cancer.

9. **Feeling anxious? Try Full Body Relaxation on page 27.** Yoga can help with being in the present moment and finding peace, which can help treat anxiety.

10. **Back pain? Body pain? Try Cat-Cow Pose on page 26.** Yoga can help reduce inflammation and improve flexibility in the body to reduce pain levels.

Source: McCall, T. (2017) 38 Health Benefits of Yoga. Yoga Journal. April 12, 2017.

Acknowledgements

Special thanks to my teacher, Amma (Sri Mata Amritanandamayi Devi). I am so grateful for her unwavering guidance, encouragement and support. Many thanks to James Fox for his vision, knowledge, and compassion. His book is a foundation for being truly free.

Thank you to all those who helped with producing this workbook: Annette Wood and Adam Olenchick, the Graphic Designers, and Rama Devi (Nina Marshall), Geoff O'Meara, Kathy Telford, Kathleen G. Mavros and Rebecca Cervenak, the editors. Also, to my wonderful family and friends who offered their unconditional love and support. Thank you to all the young men and women in juvenile prisons with whom I have worked; I admire your strength and your courage. Thank you dear readers, for reading and trying to practice these principles in your lives.

I hope this guide helps you explore all the wonderful things that are already within you. Strive for a daily practice of yoga and meditation to help you always stay centered in your highest Self no matter what is happening in your life.

May your yoga practice be blessed. May you be happy and healthy, and may the love and peace created within your heart extend out to everyone around the world.

For more information about the Prison Yoga Project, please contact us:

The Prison Yoga Project
P.O. Box 415
Bolinas, CA 94924

Dr. Lynn Williams
P.O. Box 40213
Bay Village, OH 44140

Together, may we come one step closer to making the dream of world peace come true.

Lynn Williams

Participate in one of our mindful yoga classes with our new DVD

Yoga F.L.A.M.E.: Yoga and Mind-Body Skills for Life!

Our awesome instructors videotaped a sample of our yoga classes just for you! This 2 ½ hour DVD gives an overview of our research-based, therapeutic yoga program and has two full length (45 minute) yoga classes that focus on developing skills for increased mind-body awareness (mindfulness). The goal of these exercises are to improve skills to manage stress and the way we handle our emotions and relationships. There is a bonus 30 minute relaxation class specially designed for better stress management and to improve sleep. Our yoga program addresses these five areas of greatest clinical need for those impacted by the criminal justice system.

All the exercises in this DVD are to help you recharge, reset, and restore your mind-body system for a happier, healthier you!

1 Focus:

- Increase Attention and Concentration
- Increase Energy

2 Let Go:

- Increase Relaxation
- Sleep Better

3 Anger Management:

- Improve Managing Anger
- Increase Frustration Tolerance

4 Mindfulness:

- Improve Stress Management
- Let Go of Anxiety

5 Exhale Negativity:

- Increase your Mood
- Improve Emotion Regulation

DVD segments

DISC ONE

- Chapter 1 Introduction by Golden Ciphers Executive Director, Pamela Hubbard (4 mins.)
- Chapter 2 Urban Yogis Video: Juquille's Story (7 mins.)
- Chapter 3 Welcome to Yoga: An Introduction (6 mins.)
- Chapter 4 Yoga Sequence 1: Beginner's Yoga with Dr. Chris Van Huysse (35 mins.)
- Chapter 5: Urban Yogis Video: The Horizon Story (5 mins.)
- Chapter 6: Yoga Sequence 2: Advanced Power Yoga with Judge Dawson (42 mins.)

DISC TWO: BONUS

- Chapter 7 Yoga Sequence 3: Relaxation Yoga with Dr. Lynn Williams (27 mins.)
- Chapter 8: Interviews with our Prison Yoga Team (29 mins.)

This DVD is a companion to the book, **The Power of Peace Within Me: Mindful Yoga for Healing by Dr. Lynn Williams.**

This project is a collaboration of the Golden Ciphers, Inc. Youth Development & Cultural Arts Center, Prison Yoga Project Ohio, Kodjoarts Videography, LLC and The Yoga Lab.
To purchase please contact: Dr. Lynn Williams: drlynnwilliams@gmail.com, P.O. Box 40213, Bay Village, OH 44140.

Made in the USA
Middletown, DE
06 July 2022

The Power of Peace Within Me

By Lynn Williams, PhD

Prison Yoga Project Northern Ohio Juvenile Program

www.facebook.com/prisonyoga.org
www.prisonyoga.org

Ordering Information:
Special discounts are available on quantity purchases by corporations, associations, and others. For details, contact the publisher at drlynnwilliams@gmail.com.

Cover and Interior Design: AnnetteWoodGraphics.com

Printed in the United States of America

First Printing, 2022

ISBN 978-0-578-44346-1